TWELVE BASKETS FULL

Vol. II

TWELVE
BASKETS
FULL

Vol. II

CHURCH BOOK ROOM
HONG KONG

First Published October 1966
Second Impression February 1968
Third Impression July 1968

Copies may be ordered from:

CHURCH BOOK ROOM
5, Observatory Road,
Kowloon, Hong Kong

THE STREAM PUBLISHERS
P.O. Box 20755,
Los Angeles, California 90006
U. S. A.

CHRISTIAN LITERATURE CRUSADE
Fort Washington, Penna. 19034
U. S. A.

Printed by

THE WORLD OUTREACH, Publishers
P.O. Box 13448,
Hong Kong

CONTENTS

Foreword 7

Chapter 1   Ministry to the House or to the Lord 9

Chapter 2   The Treasure in Earthen Vessels 22

Chapter 3   Two Principles of Conduct 32

Chapter 4   Expecting the Lord's Blessing 48

Chapter 5   God's Purpose and God's Rest 65

Chapter 6   Special Grace and Reserve Grace 73

Chapter 7   God's Keeping Power 89

Chapter 8   Worshipping the Ways of God 98

Chapter 9   The Key to Prayer 125

Chapter 10 Burden and Prayer 136

Chapter 11 The Life of the Altar and the Tent 145

Chapter 12 Deep Calleth Unto Deep 153

FOREWORD

This book does not present a consecutive series of addresses, but a few unrelated messages — fragments of a rich spoken ministry. As the title of the book suggests, they are reminiscent of the fragments collected after our Lord had fed the multitude. These messages which are translated from Chinese and slightly abridged and which appeared formerly in booklet form are now collected into this volume.

CHAPTER ONE

MINISTRY TO THE HOUSE OR TO THE LORD

Scripture Reading: Ezk. 44.9-26, 28, 31; Lk. 17.7-10.

Let us note at the outset that there is little apparent difference between ministry to the House and ministry to the Lord. Many of you are doing your utmost to help your brethren, and you are labouring to save sinners and administer the affairs of the church. But let me ask you: Have you been seeking to meet the need around you, or have you been seeking to serve the Lord? Is it your fellowmen you have in view, or is it Him?

Let us be quite frank. Work for the Lord undoubtedly has its attractions for the flesh. You may find it very interesting, and you may be thrilled when crowds gather to hear you preach, and when numbers of souls are saved. If you have to stay at home, occupied from morning to night with mundane matters, then you think: How meaningless life is! How grand it would be if I could go out and serve the Lord! If only I were free to go around preaching, or even to talk to people about Him!

But that is not spirituality. That is merely a matter of natural preference. Oh, if only we could see that very much work done for God is not really ministry to

Him! He Himself has told us that there was a class of
Levites who busily served in the Temple, and yet they
were not serving Him; they were merely serving the
House. Service to the Lord and service to the House
appear so much alike that it is often difficult to
differentiate between the two.

If an Israelite came along to the Temple and wanted
to worship God, those Levites would come to his aid and
help him offer his peace offering and his burnt offering.
They would help him drag the sacrifice to the altar,
and they would slay it. Surely that was a grand work
to be engaged in, reclaiming sinners and leading believers
closer to the Lord! And God took account of the service
of those Levites who helped men bring their peace
offerings and their burnt offerings to the altar. Yet He
said it was not ministry to Himself.

Brothers and Sisters, there is a heavy burden on my
heart that you might realize what God is after. He
wants ministers who will minister to Him. "They shall
come near to *Me* to minister unto *Me;* and they shall
stand before *Me* to offer unto *Me* the fat and the blood.
They shall minister unto Me."

The thing I fear most is that many of you will go
out and win sinners to the Lord and build up believers,
without ministering to the Lord Himself. Much so-
called service for Him is simply following our natural
inclinations. We have such active dispositions that we
cannot bear to stay at home, so we run around for our

own relief. We may be serving sinners, and we may be serving believers, but we are all the time serving our own flesh.

I have a dear friend who is now with the Lord. One day, after we had had a time of prayer together, we read this passage in Ezekiel (Ezk. 44.9-26, 28, 31). She was very much older than I, and she addressed me like this: "My young brother, it was twenty years ago that I first studied this passage of Scripture." "How did you react to it?" I asked. She replied: "As soon as I had finished reading it I closed my Bible, and kneeling down before the Lord I prayed: 'Lord, make me to be one who shall minister to Thee, not to the Temple'." Can we also pray that prayer?

But what do we really mean when we talk of serving God or serving the Temple? Here is what the Word says: "But the priests, the Levites, the sons of Zadok, that kept the charge of My sanctuary when the children of Israel went astray from Me, *they shall come near to Me* to minister unto Me; *and they shall stand before Me* to offer unto Me the fat and the blood, saith the Lord God." The conditions basic to all ministry that can truly be called ministry to the Lord are – drawing near to Him and standing before Him.

How hard we often find it to drag ourselves into His presence! We shrink from the solitude, and even when we do detach ourselves physically, our thoughts still keep wandering outside. Many of us can enjoy working among people, but how many of us can draw near to God in the Holy of Holies? Yet it is only as we draw near to Him that we can minister to Him. To come into the presence of God and kneel before Him for an hour demands all the strength we possess. We have to be violent to hold that ground. But every one who serves the Lord knows the preciousness of such times, the sweetness of waking at midnight and spending an hour in prayer, or waking very early in the morning and getting up for an hour of prayer before the final sleep of the night. Let me be very frank with you. Unless we really know what it is to draw near to God, we cannot know what it is to serve *Him*. It is impossible to stand afar off and still minister to *Him*. We cannot serve Him from a distance. There is only one place where ministry to Him is possible and that is the Holy Place. In the outer court you approach the people; in the Holy Place you approach the Lord.

The passage we have quoted emphasizes the need of drawing near to God if we are to minister to Him. It speaks also of standing before Him to minister. It seems to me that today we always want to be moving on; we cannot stand still. There are so many things claiming our attention that we are perpetually on the go. We cannot stop for a moment. But a spiritual person knows how to stand still. He can stand before God till

God makes His will known. He can stand and await orders.

I wish to address myself specially to my fellow-workers. May I ask you: Is not all your work definitely organized and carried out to schedule? And has it not got to be done in great haste? Can you be persuaded to call a halt and not move for a little while? That is what is referred to here—"stand and minister to Me."

None can truly minister to the Lord who do not know the meaning of this word: "They shall *draw nigh to Me* and minister unto Me." Nor can any minister to Him who do not understand this further word: "They shall *stand before Me* to minister unto Me." Brethren, do you not think any servant should await his master's orders before seeking to serve him?

There are only two types of sin before God. One is the sin of rebelling against His commands, i.e. refusing to obey when He issues orders. The other is the sin of going ahead when the Lord has not issued orders. The one is rebellion; the other is presumption. The one is not doing what the Lord has required; the other is doing what the Lord has not required. Standing before the Lord deals with the sin of doing what the Lord has not commanded.

Brothers and Sisters, how much of the work you have done has been based on the clear command of the Lord? How much have you done because of His direct instructions? And how much have you done simply on the ground that the thing you did was a good thing to do? Let me tell you that nothing so damages the Lord's interests as a 'good thing.' 'Good things' are the greatest hindrance to the accomplishment of His will. The moment we are faced with anything wicked or unclean, we immediately recognize it as a thing the Christian ought to avoid, and for that reason things which are positively evil are not such a menace to the Lord's purpose as good things. You think: This thing would not be wrong, or, That thing is the very best that could be done; so you go ahead and do it without stopping to enquire if it is the will of God. Oh! we who are His children all know that we ought not to do anything evil, but we think that if only our conscience does not forbid a thing, or if a thing commends itself to us as positively good, that is reason enough to go ahead and do it.

That thing you contemplate doing may be very good, but are you standing before the Lord awaiting His command regarding it? "They shall stand before Me" involves halting in His presence and refusing to move till He issues His orders. Ministry to the Lord means that. In the outer court it is human need that governs. Just let someone come along to sacrifice an ox or a sheep, and there is work for you to do. But in the Holiest Place there is utter solitude. Not a soul comes in. No brother or sister governs us here, nor does any committee determine our affairs. In the Holiest Place there is one authority only, the authority of the Lord. If He appoints me a task I do it; if He appoints me no task I do none.

But something is required of us as we stand before the Lord and minister to Him. We are required to offer Him "the fat and the blood." The blood answers the demands of His holiness and righteousness; the fat meets the requirements of His glory. The blood deals with the question of our sin: the fat deals with the question of His satisfaction. The blood removes all that belongs to the old creation: the fat brings in the new. And this is something more than spiritual doctrine. *Our* soul-life was involved in the pouring out of *His* soul unto the death. When He shed His eternally incorruptible blood, He was not only pouring out His own life, He was pouring out the whole of the life man had by natural birth. And He not only died: He arose from the dead, and "the life that He lives He lives unto God." He lives for God's satisfaction. He offers "the fat and the blood." We too, who would minister to the Lord, must offer the fat and the blood. And that impossible thing is possible on the basis of what He has done.

But such ministry is confined to a certain place, "They shall enter into My sanctuary, and they shall come near to My table to minister unto Me, and they shall keep My charge" (v.16). Ministry that is "unto Me" is in the inner sanctuary, in the hidden place, not in the outer court exposed to public view. People may think we are doing nothing, but service to God within the Holy

Place far transcends service to the people in the outer court. Brothers and Sisters, let us learn what it means to stand before the Lord awaiting His orders, serving at His command only, and governed by no consideration but the consideration of His will.

The same passage tells us how they must be clothed who would minister to the Lord. "They shall be clothed with linen garments; and no wool shall come upon them, whiles they minister in the gates of the inner court, and within. They shall have linen tires upon their heads, and shall have linen breeches upon their loins." Those who minister to the Lord may not wear wool. Why not? The reason is given below: "They shall not gird themselves with anything that causeth sweat." No work that produces sweat is acceptable to the Lord. But what does 'sweat' signify? We all know that the first occasion when sweat is mentioned was when Adam was driven from the garden of Eden. After Adam had sinned God pronounced this sentence upon him: "Cursed is the ground for thy sake; in toil shalt thou eat of it all the days of thy life. . . in the sweat of thy face shalt thou eat bread" (Gen. 3.17-19). It is clear that sweat is a condition of the curse. Because the curse rested on the ground it ceased to yield its fruit without man's effort, and such effort produced sweat. When the blessing of God is withheld, fleshly effort becomes necessary, and that causes sweat. All work that produces sweat is positively prohibited to those who minister to the Lord.

Yet today what an expenditure of energy there is in work for Him! Alas! few Christians can do any work today without sweating over it. Their work involves planning and scheming, exhorting and urging, and very much running around. It cannot be done without a great deal of fleshly zeal. Nowadays if there is no sweat, there is no work. Before work for God can be undertaken there is a great deal of rushing to and fro making numerous contacts, having consultations and discussions, and finally getting the approval of various people before going ahead. As for waiting quietly in the presence of God and seeking His instructions, that is out of the question. Yet in spiritual work the one factor to be taken into account is God. The one Person to make contact with is God. Oh! that is the preciousness of spiritual work—it is related to God. And in relation to Him there is work to do, but it is work that produces no sweat. If we have to advertise the work and use great effort to promote it, then it is obvious that it does not spring from prayer in the presence of God. Please bear with me when I say that all work which is truly spiritual is done in the presence of God. If you really work in God's presence, when you come into the presence of men they will respond. You will not have to use endless means in order to help them. Spiritual work is God's work, and when God works man does not need to expend so much effort that he sweats over it.

Brothers and Sisters, let us in utter honesty examine ourselves before God today. Let us ask Him: Am I serving You, or am I serving the work? Is my ministry "unto the Lord," or is it "unto the House"? If you are pouring with sweat all the time, then you yourself can come to the conclusion that it is the House you are serving, not the Lord. If all your busyness is related to human need, you may know that you are serving men, not God. I am not despising the work of slaying sacrifices at the altar. It is work for God and someone has to do it; but God wants something beyond that.

God cannot secure everyone for service to Himself, for many of His own are reluctant to leave the thrill and excitement of the outer court. They are bent on serving the people. But what about us? Oh that today we might say to the Lord: 'I am willing to forsake things, I am willing to forsake the work, I am willing to forsake the outer court and serve You in the inner sanctuary.

When God could find no way to bring all the Levites to the place of ministry to Himself, He chose the sons of Zadok from among them for this special service. Why did He select the sons of Zadok? Because, when the children of Israel went astray, they recognized that the outer court had been irreparably corrupted, so they did not seek to preserve it; but they made it their business to preserve the sanctity of the Holy Place.

Brothers and Sisters, can you bear to let the external structure go, or must you persist in putting up a scaffolding to preserve it? It is the Holy Place God is out to preserve—a place utterly set apart for Him, a place where the standard is absolute. Oh! I beseech you before God to hear His call to forsake the outer court and devote yourself to His service in the Holy Place.

I love to read in Acts 13 about the prophets and teachers in the church at Antioch, that "as they ministered to the Lord and fasted, the Holy Ghost said: Separate Me Barnabas and Saul for the work whereunto I have called them." We see there the one principle that governs work for God in the New Testament dispensation. The Holy Spirit only commissions men to the work as they are ministering to the Lord. Unless ministry to the Lord is the thing that governs us, the work will be in confusion. In the beginning of the church's history in Antioch, the Holy Spirit said: "Separate *Me* Barnabas and Saul for the work whereunto *I* have called them." God does not want volunteers for His work; He wants conscripts. He will not have you preaching the Gospel just because you want to. The work of the Lord is suffering serious damage today at the hand of volunteers; it lacks those who can say as He did: "He that sent Me. . ." Oh! Brothers and Sisters, the work of God is God's own work, and not work that you can take up at your pleasure. Neither churches, nor missionary societies, nor evangelistic bands can send men to work for God. The authority to commission men is not in the hands of men, but solely in the hands of the Spirit of God.

Serving the Lord does not mean that we do not serve our fellow-men, but it does mean that all service to men has service to the Lord as its basis. It is service Godward that urges us out manward.

Luke 17.7-10 tells us clearly what the Lord is after. These are two kinds of work referred to here—ploughing the field and tending the flock—both very important occupations; yet the Lord says that even when a servant returns from such work, he is expected to provide for his master's satisfaction before sitting down to enjoy his own food. When we have returned from our toil in the field we are apt to muse complacently on the much work we have accomplished; but the Lord will say: "Gird yourself and give Me to eat." He requires ministry to Himself. We may have laboured in a wide field and cared for many sheep; but all our toil in the field and among the flock does not exempt us from ministry to the Lord's own personal satisfaction. That is our supreme task.

Brothers and Sisters, what are we really after? Is it only work in the field, only preaching the Gospel to the unsaved? Is it just tending the flock, just caring for the needs of the saved? Or are we seeing to it that the Lord can eat to His full satisfaction and drink till His thirst is quenched? True, it is necessary for us also to eat and drink, but that cannot be till after the Lord is satisfied. We too must have our enjoyment, but that can never be until His joy is full. Let us ask ourselves:

Does our work minister to our satisfaction or to the Lord's? I fear that when we have worked for the Lord, we are often thoroughly satisfied before He is satisfied. We are often quite happy with our work when He has found no joy in it.

Brothers and Sisters, when you and I have done our utmost, we still have to admit that we are unprofitable servants. Our goal is not ministry to the world, nor to the Church, but ministry to the Lord. And blessed are they who can differentiate between ministry to sinners or saints, and ministry to Him. Such discernment is not easily acquired. Only by much drastic dealing shall we learn the difference between ministry to the Lord Himself and ministry to the House.

Nevertheless, if the Holy Spirit has His way in our lives, He will prove equal to the need. Let us seek grace of God that He may reveal to us what it really means to minister to Him!

CHAPTER TWO

THE TREASURE IN EARTHEN VESSELS

Scripture Reading: II Corinthians 1.8, 9; 4.7-10; 6.8-10;
12.7-10.

THE PAUL OF II CORINTHIANS.

As we read II Corinthians carefully we seem to meet two persons—Paul in himself and Paul in Christ. Everything Paul speaks of, from the opening chapter of this epistle to its conclusion, is in one strain. There is one governing principle throughout, which we might summarise in his own words: "We have this treasure in earthen vessels." In the very first chapter we see "this treasure" in an earthen vessel; and right to the last chapter we keep meeting the earthen vessel, yet we keep meeting the treasure too.

II Corinthians is the most personal of the New Testament books. Other epistles bring the revelation of God to us, but II Corinthians is unique in this respect that it shews us the kind of man he is through whom God imparts His revelation. Had we not this epistle we might still know what work Paul accomplished, but we should not know what kind of man he was who accomplished the work. He was an earthen vessel.

THE IDEAL CHRISTIAN

When I first became a Christian I had my own conception as to what a Christian was, and I tried my utmost to be that kind of Christian. I thought, if only I could attain to the standard I had conceived, then I should have attained perfection. To be perfect was my ambition, but I had my own mentality as to the standard of perfection. I thought a perfect Christian should smile from morning to night; if at any time he shed a tear he had ceased to be victorious. I thought a perfect Christian must be a very courageous person; if under any circumstances he showed the slightest sign of fear then I said he lacked faith, he could not trust the Lord, he was not perfect.

PAUL WAS A MAN

I retained these clearly defined ideas as to what a Christian should be like until, one day as I was reading II Corinthians, I came to the passage where Paul said he was sad. I was arrested. Paul sad? I thought. Then I read that he shed many tears, and I thought, Can it actually be that Paul wept? I read that he was pressed, that he was perplexed; and I thought, Was Paul really pressed? Was Paul really perplexed? This also I read: "We were weighed down exceedingly, beyond our power, so that we despaired even of life." And I wondered, Can it be that Paul despaired? It had never occurred to me that a person like Paul could have experiences such as these. But as I read on I gradually awakened to the fact that Christians are not another order of angelic beings, and that Paul was not so very remote from us. In fact, I discovered that Paul was a man and that he was the very kind of man I know.

Here is a man who is afraid, yet he is strong: he is encompassed by foes, yet he is not bound: he looks as though he is overcome, yet he is not destroyed. You can see he is weak, yet he declares that when he is weak he is strong. You can see that he bears in his body the dying of Jesus, yet he says the life of Jesus is also manifested in his body. You hear his "evil report", but you also hear his "good report". He appears to be a "deceiver", nevertheless he is "true". He seems to be "unknown", yet he is "well known". He is as one "dying" and still he "lives". He is "as sorrowful, yet alway rejoicing: as poor, yet making many rich: as having nothing, yet possessing all things". Here is a Christian!

A SPIRITUAL PARADOX

Do you realise what it means to be a Christian? To be a Christian is to be a person in whom there is a fundamental inconsistency. A Christian is one in whom there is an inherent paradox. This paradox is of God. Some people conceive of Christianity as being all treasure and no earthen vessel. If they meet the earthen vessel anywhere, they feel things are all wrong. But God's conception is totally different from man's. Here is God's thought: "We have this treasure in earthen vessels." So it is not a hopeless case if the earthen vessel is in evidence. God's purpose does not nullify the earthen vessel; it puts the treasure there. It is always in the earthen vessel that the treasure is found.

Let me say that there is not a soul whose earthen vessel is so earthen that the treasure cannot appear in it. The beauty of the treasure is enhanced by the earthen vessel in which it is placed. Paul was a man, a real man, but the life of the Lord shone out through his life. He was not an automaton; he had feelings. And he was neither invariably sorrowful, nor was he invariably glad. At the very time when he was sorrowful he was also glad. It is characteristic of Christianity that even while the tears flow the face can relax into a smile.

We keep hoping that when we meet Christians we shall see no trace of the earthen vessel, yet when we meet some of the Lord's truest children we immediately recognise their distinctive personalities. We recognise what kind of persons they are in themselves and also what kind of persons they are in the Lord. I knew a sister who had a very quick temper. She was quick at everything—quick to speak, quick to rebuke, quick to write letters, and quick to destroy the letters she wrote. You could see at once what sort of person she was, yet at the same time you could see the Lord in her. You could see her suffering under trial, but at the same time you could see her spiritual wealth. You could see the treasure in an earthen vessel.

Many people tell me they have prayed for a certain thing; they affirm they have faith in God and are absolutely certain He has heard their prayer and granted their request. Yet nothing happens. Why? Because their faith is too wonderful. The treasure is not in an earthen vessel.

Many other people have come to me and told of their fears and misgivings even while they sought to trust the Lord. They made their requests, and they laid hold of the promises of God; yet doubts continually arose unbidden. Let me tell you that true faith cannot be killed by doubt. The treasure of true faith appears in an earthen vessel of doubt, and the earthen vessel does not nullify the treasure. In such an environment the treasure shines forth with enhanced beauty. Do not misunderstand me, I am not encouraging doubt; but I do wish to make this clear, that Christianity is not a matter of treasure only, nor of earthen vessels only, but of treasure in earthen vessels.

I love to recall the prayer of the early church for Peter's deliverance from the hands of wicked men. When Peter returned and knocked at the door the believers said it was his angel. Do you see? There was faith there, true faith, the kind of faith that could bring an answer from God; but the weakness of man was still present, and that weakness was clearly manifest. Today the faith exercised by many of God's people is greater than that exercised by the believers gathered in the house of Mary, the mother of John Mark. And they are so positive about it. They are certain God will send an angel, and every door in the prison will swing open. If a gust of wind blows, there is Peter knocking at the door! If the rain begins to patter, there is Peter knocking at the door again! Those people are too credulous; their faith is not the genuine article. In Christianity the earthen vessel is always in evidence, though the question is never one of the earthen vessel but of the treasure within it. In the life of a normal Christian, just when faith rises positively to lay hold of God, a question may simultaneously arise as to whether he might perhaps be mistaken. When he is strongest in the Lord he is often most conscious of inability: when he is most courageous he becomes aware of fear within: when he is most joyful a sense of distress breaks upon him. This paradox is evidence that there is treasure in the earthen vessel.

GOD'S POWER IS MANIFEST
IN MAN'S WEAKNESS

Paul tells us that he had a thorn in the flesh. What that thorn was I do not know, but I do know that it was a weakening factor and that Paul prayed three times for its removal. But God answered: "My grace is sufficient for thee, for my power is made perfect in weakness." How can the Lord's power be manifested to perfection in a weak man? Christianity is that very thing. Christianity is not the removal of weakness, nor is it merely the manifestation of divine power; it is the manifestation of divine power in human weakness. Christianity does not bring in a marvellous new order of angelic beings, but human beings in whose weakness the divine power is displayed. Let me use an illustration.

I was once seriously ill. During a period of two months I was x-rayed three times, and each time the report was very grave. I prayed, and I believed. I had hoped God would heal my sickness, but though several times I experienced a great increase of strength, the root of the trouble remained, so the possibility of relapse was always present. I was annoyed. What was the use of a temporary increase of strength? One day, as I was reading the Bible, I came to the chapter in II Corinthians where Paul prayed three times that God would remove his "thorn". God would not do so, but said: "My grace is sufficient for thee." Because of the presence of the thorn he was granted an increase of grace. Because the weakness persisted, grace was added. I saw —This is Christianity! I prayed for a clearer seeing, and the thought came to me of a boat that could not pass because of a boulder jutting out five feet from the river bed. I had been praying in effect: "Lord, if it please Thee, remove the boulder." Now a question arose within: Whether would it be better to have the five foot boulder removed, or to let the Lord raise the level of the water by five feet? I answered: It would be better to have the level of the water raised. From that day many of my difficulties were gone. I dare not say that I was never tempted; but, praise God! I discovered that He has resource to deal with difficulties other than by their removal. Christianity is not a matter of removing boulders, but of raising the level of the water. Have you difficulties? Yes. Have you weaknesses? Yes, we all have. But do bear in mind that what the Lord is after is not, on the negative side, the removal of our weaknesses; nor is it even, on the positive side, the indiscriminate bestowal of strength. All the strength He gives is manifest in weakness. All the treasure we have is in earthen vessels.

MAN'S WEAKNESS DOES NOT LIMIT GOD'S POWER

It is cause for great gratitude to God that no human weakness need limit the divine power. We are apt to think that where sadness exists, there joy cannot exist: that where there are tears there cannot be praise: that where weakness is present power must be absent: that where there is doubt there cannot be faith. But let me proclaim this with a clear voice, that God is seeking to bring us to the point where we recognise that all that is of man is only intended to provide an earthen vessel to contain the divine treasure. Henceforth when we are conscious of depression let us not give way to

depression, but to the Lord; and the treasure will shine
forth all the more gloriously because of the earthen
vessel. I am not theorising here; I know what I am
talking about. Herein lies the glory of Christianity, that
God's treasure can be manifest in every earthen vessel.
Christianity is a paradox, and it is as we Christians live
this paradoxical life that we get to know God. The
further we go on in the Christian life, the more paradoxical it becomes. The treasure becomes increasingly
manifest, but the earthen vessel is the earthen vessel
still. This is very beautiful. Just look at the divine
patience in a man who by nature is impatient, and
compare the sight of that with a man whom nothing
can ever move. See the divine humility in one who
by nature is haughty, and compare that with one who
is always of a retiring disposition. See the strength of
God in a person of weak temperament, and compare
that with a naturally strong character. The difference
is tremendous.

People who are naturally weak are always apt to
think they are no good because of the earthen quality
of the vessel; but there is no need for dejection since
the treasure within the vessel is of such a quality as to
shine forth with added splendour from within such a
vessel. Brothers and Sisters, let me say once again that
the whole question is one of the quality of the treasure,
not of the quality of the vessel that contains it. It is
folly to stress the negative aspect: our concern is with

the positive. The Lord is able to manifest Himself in the life of every one of us, and when that comes to pass many will behold the treasure.

CHAPTER THREE

TWO PRINCIPLES OF CONDUCT

Scripture Reading: 2 Cor. 5.7; Matt. 17.3, 5, 8;
1 Cor. 4.3, 4; Gen. 2.8, 9, 16, 17.

God created man, and He Who created man made provision for the sustenance of the man He had created. Man derived his existence from God, and it was God's intention that man should be dependent on Him for his life throughout its entire course. The life He had given was to be nourished by means of suitable food which He Himself supplied.

"And the Lord God planted a garden eastward, in Eden; and there he put the man whom he had formed. And out of the ground made the Lord God to grow every tree that is pleasant to the sight, and good for food; and the tree of life also in the midst of the garden, and the tree of the knowledge of good and evil" (Gen. 2.8, 9). Through these two trees God has shown us in figure two different ways in which people may spend their days on earth: the principle that governs the conduct of some is the knowledge of good and evil, while others are governed by the principle of life.

Let us spend a little time this morning considering these two different principles as they affect the lives of God's children: and let us note at the outset that while Christians may be governed mainly by the one principle or the other, not all the actions of the same Christian are invariably regulated by the same principle.

WHAT IS THE PRINCIPLE OF
GOOD AND EVIL?

If our conduct is controlled by the principle of good and evil, then whenever we have to make a decision we first enquire: Is this right, or is it wrong? Would it be good to do this, or would it be evil? Many Christians hesitate before doing anything and turn such questions round and round in their minds. They are bent on doing the right thing: they wish to avoid all evil: they want to live a life in keeping with what they consider to be Christianity: so they scrupulously weigh all their actions. They carefully examine each situation they meet, and not until they are persuaded that a certain course of action is good will they go ahead. They seek to act in a way that befits a Christian, so they are always on the alert to select the right from the wrong and to do only what they consider to be right.

But God's Word says: "The tree of the knowledge of good and evil, thou shalt not eat of it: for in the day that thou eatest thereof thou shalt surely die." To act according to the seemingly lofty standard of rejecting

all that is bad and choosing only the good is not
Christianity.   That is living under the law: it is acting
according to the Old Covenant, not the New.   To act
in this way is to conform to religious or ethical standards:
it falls altogether short of the Christian standard.

CHRISTIANITY IS BASED ON LIFE

What is Christianity?   Christianity is a matter of
life.   If you are a Christian, then you possess a new life;
and when you have to decide on a course of action, you
do not ask, Would it be right to do this?   You ask,
If I do this, how will it affect my inner life?   How
will that new life within me react to this?   It is a most
amazing thing that the objective of so many Christians
is only conformity to an external standard, though what
God has given us by new birth is not a lot of new rules
and regulations to which we are required to conform.
He has not brought us to a new Sinai and given us a
new set of commandments with their "Thou shalt" and
"Thou shalt not."   Christianity does not require that
we investigate the rights and wrongs of alternative
courses of action, but that we test the reaction of the
divine life to any proposed course.   As a Christian you
now possess the life of Christ, and it is the reactions of
His life that you have to consider.   If, when you
contemplate any move, there is a rise of life within you
to make that move; if there is a positive response from
the inner life; if there is "the anointing" within (1

John 2.20, 27); then you can confidently pursue the proposed course. The inner life has indicated that. But if, when you contemplate a certain move, the inner life begins to languish, then you may know that the move you contemplated should be avoided, however commendable it may seem to be.

Do realize that the conduct of many a non-Christian is governed by the principle of right and wrong. Wherein does the Christian differ from the non-Christian if the same principle governs both? God's Word shows us plainly that the Christian is controlled by the life of Christ, not by any external code of ethics. There is something vital within the Christian that responds to what is of God and reacts against what is not of Him; so we must take heed to our inner reactions. When the living spring within us wells up in response to any suggestion, we should follow that; but when it declines, we should repudiate the idea. We dare not be governed by externalities, nor by reasonings, our own or other peoples'. Others may approve a certain thing, and when we weigh up the pros and cons we too may think it right; but what is the inner life saying about it?

THE TRANSCENDENT STANDARD OF LIFE

Once you realize that the determining factor in all Christian conduct is life, then you know that you must not only avoid all that is evil, but also all that is just externally good. Only what issues from the Christian life is Christian conduct; therefore we cannot consent to any action that does not spring from life. Let us remember God's Word: "Of the tree of the knowledge of good and evil, thou shalt not eat of it: for in the day that thou eatest thereof thou shalt surely die." Note that "good and evil" are set together here, and over against "good and evil" is set "life". The standard of life is a transcendent standard.

In my early Christian days I sedulously sought to avoid all that was evil and deliberately set myself to do what was good. And I seemed to be making splendid progress. At that time I had a fellowworker who was two years older than I, and we two were always disagreeing. The differences that arose between us were not concerning our own personal affairs: our disagreements were about public matters and our disputes were public too. I used to say to myself: If he wants to do that bit of work in such-and-such a way I shall protest, for it is not right. But no matter how I protested, he always refused to give way. I had one line of argument—right and wrong: he also had one line of argument—his seniority. No matter how I might reason in support of my views, he invariably reasoned that he was two years older than I. However many irrefutable evidences I might produce to prove that he was wrong and I was right, he produced his one unvarying evidence to justify every course of action he adopted—he was two years older than I. How could I refute that fact?

So he always won the day. He gained his point outwardly, but inwardly I never gave way. I resented his unreasonableness and still clung firmly to my contention that he was wrong and I was right. One day I brought my grievance to an elderly sister in the Lord who had a wealth of spiritual experience. I explained the case, brought forth my arguments, then appealed to her to arbitrate. Was he right or was I?—that was what I wanted to know. She seemed to ignore all the rights and wrongs of the situation, and looking me straight in the face, just answered quietly, "You'd better do as he says." I was thoroughly dissatisfied with her answer and thought to myself: If I'm right, why not acknowledge that I'm right? If I'm wrong, why not tell me I'm wrong? Why tell me to do what he says? So I asked, "Why?" "Because", she said, "in the Lord the younger should submit to the old." "But", I retorted, "in the Lord, if the younger is right and the older wrong, must the younger still submit?" At that time I was a high school student and had learned nothing of discipline, so I gave free vent to my annoyance. She simply smiled and said once more: "You'd better do as he says."

At a later date there was to be a baptismal service and three of us were to bear responsibility together— the brother who was two years older than I, a brother who was seven years older than he, and myself. Now let's see what will happen, I thought. I always have to do what you, who are my senior by two years, tell me:

will you always do what this brother, who is your senior by seven years, tells you? Together we three discussed the work, but he refused to accept any suggestion put forward by his senior: at every point he insisted on having his own way. Finally he dismissed us both with the remark: "You two just leave things to me; I can manage quite well alone." I thought, What kind of logic is this? You insist that I always obey you because you are my senior, but you need never obey your senior. Forthwith I sought out the elderly sister, spread the matter before her, and asked for her verdict on the case. "The thing that annoys me", I said, "is that that brother has no place for right and wrong." She rose to her feet and asked: "Have you, right up to this present day, never seen what the life of Christ is? These past few months you keep asserting that you are right and your brother is wrong. Do you not know the meaning of the Cross?" Since the one issue I raised was the issue of right or wrong, she met me on my own ground and asked: "Do you think it right for you to behave as you have been doing? Do you think it right for you to talk as you have been talking? Do you think it right for you to come and report these matters to me? You may be acting reasonably and rightly; but even if you are, what about your inner registrations? Does the life within you not protest against your own behaviour?" I had to admit that even when I was right by human standards, the inner life pronounced me wrong.

The Christian standard not only passes its verdict
on what is not good, but also on that which is mere
external goodness. Many things are right according to
human standards, but the divine standard pronounces
them wrong because they lack the divine life. On the
day to which I have just referred I saw for the first time
that if I was to live in the presence of God, then all my
conduct must be governed by the principle of life, not
by the principle of right and wrong. From that day I
began to see more and more clearly that in relation to
any course of action, even if others pronounced it right,
and I myself considered it right, and every aspect of
the case indicated that it was right, I must still be very
sensitive to the reactions of the life of Christ within me.
As we advance in the approved course, does the inner
life grow stronger or weaker? Does the inner
"anointing" confirm the rightness of the course, or does
an absence of the "anointing" indicate that the divine
approval is withheld? God's way for us is not known
by external indications but by internal registrations. It
is peace and joy in the spirit that indicate the Christian's
path.

When I was visiting a certain place, a brother who
was exceedingly critical of the place was a guest there
too. He knew the place had much to offer spiritually,
but disapproved of very much that was done there and
was constantly making adverse comparisons with the
place form which he came. During the two or three

months we were there together his criticisms exceeded
those of everyone else. One day he went altogether too
far, so I said to him: "Why ever do you remain here?
Why not pack up and leave?" "The reason lies here",
he answered, pointing to his heart. "Every time I
prepare to go, my peace of heart goes. Once I actually
departed, and I stayed away for a fortnight, but I had
to ask to be allowed to return." "Brother," I said,
"can't you see these two different lines of conduct—
that which is determined by life and that which is
determined by right and wrong?" "Oh!" he said, "not
once or twice merely, but a number of times I have
sought to leave here, and every time my experience has
been the same; as soon as I prepare to go there is an
inner forbidding. Even if much that is done here is
wrong, for me to leave is also wrong." This brother
saw that if there was much spiritual help to be gained
in that place, then his only way was to remain there and
meet God.

EXTERNALITIES DO NOT GOVERN DECISIONS

One of the most serious misconceptions among the
children of God is that actions are determined by right
and wrong. They do what their eyes tell them is right:
they do what their background tells them is right: they
do what their years of experience tell them is right.
For a Christian, every decision should be based on the
inner life, and that is something totally different from

all else. I yearn that you should come to see that a
Christian should arrive at no decision other than that
which is dictated by life. If the life within you rises
to do a thing, then it is right for you to do it: if the
life within shrinks back when you advance, then you
should immediately call a halt.

I can recall going to a certain place where the
brothers were working to real effect. God was truly
using them. If you were to ask: Was their work
perfect? I should have to answer, No, there was
lots of room for improvement. In great humility they
asked me to point out anything I saw that was not
correct, so I pointed out this and that. But no change
took place. Was I annoyed? Not at all. I could only
indicate external matters that called for adjustment: I
could not see what God was doing inwardly, and it
would have been folly on my part to touch that. I
dared not advise God what to do in their lives.

In another place I visited, the brothers were not
preaching the gospel. They discussed the matter with
me and asked if I did not think they ought to be doing
so. "Doctrinally you certainly ought", I answered. They
admitted that they felt the same, but the surprising thing
was that God did not give them the life to do so.
Under such circumstances, if we know God we can only
stand aside in silence, for our pathway is governed by
His life alone, not by right and wrong. Brothers and
Sisters, the contrast between these two principles of life

is immense. So many people are still questioning: "Is it right for me to do this? Would it be wrong for me to do that?" The one question for the Christian to ask is, Does the divine life within me rise or fall when I contemplate this thing? The reaction of the divine life within me must determine the course I follow at every point. This is a heart matter.

"HEAR HIM"

On the Mount of Transfiguaration Moses was present, representing the law; and Elijah was present, representing the prophets. The legal standard was there, and the prophetic standard was there too: but the two who throughout the Old Testament dispensation were qualified to speak were put to silence by God. "This is my beloved Son"; He said, "hear ye him." Today the standard for the Christian is neither the law nor the prophets; it is Christ, the Christ Who dwells within us: therefore the question is not, Am I right or am I wrong? but, Does the divine life in me acquiesce to this? We shall often find that what we ourselves approve of the life within us disapproves. When that is so, we cannot do what we thought right.

THE DIVINE LIFE MUST BE SATISFIED

I recall a story of two brothers who both cultivated paddy-fields. Their fields were half way up the hill:

others were lower down. In the great heat they drew water by day and went to sleep at night. One night, while they were sleeping, the farmers lower down the hill dug a hole in the irrigation channel surrounding the brothers' fields and let all the water flow down on their own fields. Next morning the brothers saw what had happened, but said nothing. Again they filled the troughs with water, and again all the water was drawn off the following night. Still no word of protest was uttered when the next day dawned and they discovered what a mean trick the same farmers had played on them. Were they not Christians? Ought not Christians to be patient? This game was repeated seven nights in succession; and for seven days in succession these two brothers silently suffered the wrong. One would have thought that Christians who could allow themselves to be treated like that day after day, and never utter a word of reproach, would surely be overflowing with joy. Strange to say, they were not happy at all, and their unhappiness distressed them to such an extent that they brought the matter to a brother who was in the Lord's service. Having stated their case, they asked him: "How does it come about that, having suffered all this wrong for a full week, we are still unhappy?" This brother had some experience and he replied: "You're unhappy because you've not gone the full length. You should first irrigate those farmers' fields and then irrigate your own. You go back and test it out, and see whether

off they went. Next morning they were afoot earlier
or not your hearts find rest." They agreed to try, and
than ever, and their first business was to irrigate the
fields of those farmers who had so persistently robbed
their fields of water. And this amazing thing happened
—the more they laboured on their persecutors' land,
the happier they became. By the time they had finished
watering their own land their hearts were at perfect rest.
When the brothers had repeated this for two or three
days, the farmers called to apologize and added: "If
this is Christianity, then we want to hear more about it."

Here we see the difference between the principle
of right and wrong and the principle of life. Those
two brothers had been most patient: was that not right?
They had laboured in the intense heat to irrigate their
paddy-fields and without a word of complaint had
suffered others to steal their water: was that not very
good? What then was lacking that they had no peace
of heart? They had done what was right: they had
done what was good: they had done all that man could
require of them: but God was not satisfied. They had
no peace of heart because they had not met the demands
of His life. When they conformed to His standard, joy
and peace welled up in their hearts. The demands of
the divine life must be met, so we dare not stop short
of God's satisfaction.

What is the Sermon on the Mount? What is taught
us in Matthew chapters 5-7? Is it not this, that we

dare not be satisfied with anything less than that which
meets the demands of the life that God has put within
us? The Sermon on the Mount does not teach that,
provided we do what is right, then all is well. Man
would say: If anyone smites you on the one cheek, why
present the other? Surely you have attained the utmost
degree of forbearance if you take such an offence without
retort. But God says otherwise. If, when you are
smitten on the one cheek, you do no more than bow your
head and depart, you will find that the inner life will
not be satisfied. There will be no inner satisfaction till
you turn the other cheek to the smiter for the same
treatment. To do so will prove that there is no resent-
ment within. That is the way of life.

Many people say that Matthew 5-7 is too difficult;
it is beyond us. I admit it is. It is a sheer impossibility.
But here is the point—you have an inner life, and that
life tells you that unless you do as the Sermon on the
Mount requires, you will find no rest. The whole
question lies here, are you walking in the way of life or
in the way of good and evil?

THERE SHOULD BE FULNESS OF LIFE WITHIN

Sometimes a brother acts very foolishly. You feel
his actions call for strong exhortation or even serious
reproof, so one day you set out for his home. Yes, you
must give him a good talking-to: that is only right: he
has been very wrong. You reach the door: you raise

your hand to the doorbell: just as you are about to ring, your hand falls limp by your side. But, you ask, isn't it right to talk to him? The question is not whether it's right to talk to him, but whether the divine life within you allows you to do so. You may exhort that brother, and he may receive your exhortation with courtesy and promise to do what God says, but the more you preach to him the more the life within you wilts. When you return home you will have to admit, I have done wrong.

One day I met a needy brother. He was extremely poor, and there was no prospect of help coming to him from any direction, so I thought I certainly must do something for him. Just at that point I myself had no superabundance, so it was at great sacrifice that I came to his aid. I should have been full of joy when I parted with my much-needed money, but the reverse was the case. I felt lifeless, and a voice within said: You were not acting in life; you were just acting on the ground of natural kindness and responding to human need. God did not ask that of you. When I reached home I had to confess my sin and ask His forgiveness.

OUR ACTIONS MUST BE CONTROLLED BY LIFE

Brothers and Sisters, let me repeat that all our conduct must be determined, not by good and evil, but by the life within. If you act apart from the requirement of that life, even if what you do is good, you will meet with the divine reproof. We need to discern between life and death. If what I have done has sapped my inner life, however good the deed may be, I shall have to acknowledge my sin before God and seek His pardon. In 1 Cor. 4.4 Paul said: "I know nothing against myself; yet am I not hereby justified: but he that judgeth me is the Lord."   It is easy to distinguish between good and evil, but Paul was not governed by good and evil: even when he was unaware of having done anything wrong, he still did not dare affirm that all was right with him: he acknowledged that the Lord was his judge. At the judgmentseat it is the Lord Who will judge us, but His life is in us now and is directing our way. For that reason Paul said in 2 Cor. 5.7, "We walk by faith, not by sight."   We do not come to decisions on the basis of an outward, legal standard, but on the basis of an inner life. It is a fact that the Lord Jesus Christ dwells within the believer, and He is constantly express- ing Himself in us, so we must become sensitive to His life and learn to discern what that life is saying.   A great change will take place in us when our conduct is no longer governed by the principle of good and evil but only by the principle of life.

CHAPTER FOUR

EXPECTING THE LORD'S BLESSING

Scripture Reading: Matt. 14.17-21; Rom. 9.13-16.

Of late the thought has been constantly with me that all God's work is dependent on His blessing. Often we work faithfully, but despite all our faithfulness there is little result. We apply ourselves with diligence to the task, but all our diligence is unproductive. We exercise faith and we give ourselves to prayer, but our efforts are largely ineffective. Where does the trouble lie? It lies here—we lack the blessing of the Lord.

We who serve Him must learn to look to Him for His blessing. Without that our faithfulness, our diligence, our faith and our prayers will be unavailing; but with that, even if our work is faulty and our faith feeble, we shall not labour in vain. Everything in our service for the Lord is dependent on His blessing.

The feeding of the multitude illustrates this truth. The supply was totally inadequate to meet the demand; nevertheless, the demand was met. The meeting of need is not dependent on the supply in hand, but on the blessing of the Lord resting on the supply. Five loaves and two fishes proved more than sufficient to feed the five thousand people who followed Him to the desert because He blessed the food; but ten times that amount, or a hundred times, would have been insufficient without His blessing. No matter how many the gifts or how great the power we may be able to produce from our store, the need of the multitudes will not be met by these alone. The blessing of the Lord is the determining factor. When this truth breaks upon us we shall hand over what we have to Him—whether it be two loaves or a hundred and shall acknowledge: "Lord, it is Thy blessing alone that matters." It is of fundamental importance that we realise this. Whether our loaves be few or many is of little consequence. If man's hunger is to be satisfied one thing is needful. That one thing is the blessing of the Lord.

It is out of deep heart exercise that I ask this question: Do we really prize the Lord's blessing? This question is a vital one in all our work for Him. Today the situation is much more challenging than it was when His disciples with five loaves and two fishes fed the five thousand. We are confronted by a multitude vastly more numerous. With today's greater demand, and perhaps a lesser supply than then, how can the need ever be met? If we draw on our own resources they will steadily dwindle, and we shall be reduced to hopelessness when they run out. In that day we shall know that we can of ourselves do nothing.

Have you noted that the Gospels record two miracles of the feeding of a great company of people?

Why two? The two were almost identical in nature and also in the way they were performed. Why then have we the account of five thousand being fed on one occasion and of four thousand being fed on another ocasion? Why is it that the Word of God records two so similar miracles for our instruction? Is it not because of our slowness to learn a lesson of urgent importance? So many of us, instead of looking to the Lord to bless the loaves, are looking at the loaves in our hands. They are so pitifully few and so pitifully small. We gaze at them, and we calculate and calculate, and we keep wondering how they can ever meet the need. And the more we calculate, and the more we wonder, the more laborious our attempts become to feed the hungry crowds, and at times we become so exhausted with the strain that the work is brought to a standstill.

I am comforted when I recall what a brother once said. It was this: "If God wants to perform a small miracle He places us in difficult circumstances: if He wants to perform a mighty miracle He places us in impossible circumstances." Today we find ourselves in an extremely difficult situation, yes, even an impossible one. Shall we then, like the small boy, bring our scanty supply to the Lord? Our one hope in face of today's immense need is that He will perform a miracle, and that He will do it by taking the bread into His hands and blessing it.

Brothers and Sisters, those miracles of the feeding of the multitudes were the fruit of the Lord's blessing.

His blessing multiplied the loaves. And we shall see similar miracles when we cease to look at our resources and turn our gaze on the Lord. It was because the divine blessing rested on the meagre human supply that the four thousand were fed, and the five thousand too. Without it "two hundred pennyworth of bread" would not have sufficed. Through these two similar miracles our Lord sought to teach His disciples the vital lesson of looking to Him for His blessing.

When we are in difficulties, and even impossible situations, we often find to our amazement that we are carried through. It is the Lord's blessing that does it. Given that, nothing is too hard: failing that, nothing can be accomplished. When the Lord in His goodness brings us to a totally new position where we recognise the paramount importance of His blessing, then a way will be open for Him to work. Otherwise we shall remain in the same old position with the same old complaint that two hundred pennyworth of bread will be insufficient to meet the need. We shall go on deploring our inadequacy, and declaring that we have neither money enough nor men enough and on that account the work cannot be done. Neither of these constitute the real problem. The basic trouble is that we lack the Lord's blessing.

Brethren, if only we came to recognise that in God's work everything hinges on His blessing, it would bring a radical change into all our service for Him. We should then cease to reckon in terms of men, and money and bread, and we should be constantly expecting Him to make good every lack. His blessing transcends all our deficiencies. Once this truth really grips us we shall discard as worthless all our clever ways, and specious words and scrupulous work. When we set store by the blessing of the Lord and keep looking for that alone, even if we are not over punctilious about the work, and even if at times we make mistakes, we shall find that the need of the hungry is being met. We definitely hope we shall be preserved from mistakes and from careless words and acts; but we shall find that with God's blessing upon us even our serious blunders do not ultimately hinder His purpose. When He blesses the work nothing can wreck it, for the transforming power of His blessing turns liabilities into positive assets.

.Today it should be our main concern so to live that God will not have to withdraw His blessing. On the one hand we must learn to rely upon it: on the other hand we must learn to deal with everything that would hinder it. He will withhold no good thing from us while we provide Him with the required condition. When we find that the saints are not progressing spiritually and the number of the unsaved is not on the increase, let us not blame circumstances or attempt to find any other objective explanation for the lack. Rather let us be swift to acknowledge that the trouble may rest with us. If only we give God a clear way we shall experience His blessing in overflowing measure. It was said to God's people of old: "Prove me now herewith, saith the Lord of hosts, if I will not open you the windows of heaven and pour you out a blessing that there shall not be room enough to receive it." And God's word holds good today. The normal life of a Christian is a blessed life, and the work of a Christian is a blessed work. If our experience contradicts this, we should come to the Lord to discover the cause.

With the passing years it becomes more and more evident that some brothers are in the good of God's blessing while others are not. It is not that we of ourselves are able to form any judgment in this matter, but over the years the fact has become so patent that we know beforehand if one brother goes out on ministry there will certainly be fruit, whereas if another brother goes out there will be none. We can forecast the result in either case.

There is nothing arbitrary about the blessing of the Lord. It follows a specific course. It is subject to definite conditions. God finds His pleasure in one state of things while another state of things provokes His displeasure. He has His own reasons for His selection of one person and His rejection of another. If anyone fails to receive His blessing there is a sure cause. So if we go unblessed at any time, may we earnestly seek His face and ask Him to locate the trouble. If we make this a heart matter, there is hope for the future of the work; otherwise the prospect is not bright. I yearn that we may live the rest of our days on the earth ceaselessly expecting the divine blessing. Nothing will so vitally affect the work, for it is that alone that produces fruit.

I am well aware that we all have our own particular weaknesses. Some of these God seems to overlook, but there are others He will not tolerate, and where these exist His blessing cannot rest. Let us be on the alert lest we go unblessed because we persistently ignore certain weaknesses in our lives. We cannot expect to be free of all frailty, but we can seek God's mercy so that we may abide continually in the way of blessing. Shall we come to Him and say: "Lord, this vessel is weak, but forbid that it should be too shallow to contain Thy blessing. We cast ourselves on Thy mercy and trust that, though we are weak by nature, we may be saved from all weakness that would unfit us to be vessels for Thy blessing."

Oh, that blessing might stream from our lives as it streamed from the life of Abraham! May we live in a tide of blessing. May blessing become our habitat. Then we shall live in a state of constant expectancy. I believe God is wanting us to prepare for a new release in gospel work, and we are in danger of setting a limit to what He would do. One of the most serious threats to future blessing is past blessing. It is sadly possible for our satisfaction over the thousand souls that have come to the Lord to be the thing that hinders the unsaved coming to Him in tens of thousands. Every blessing He gives should pave the way for further blessing; it should never become a barrier to the greater grace He waits to bestow. We must ceaselessly advance, planting our feet firmly in the way of fuller and ever fuller blessing—yes, unprecedented blessing. Right ahead of us lies a work immensely greater than that which lies behind us. Is it not possible that the large hall we have built for the proclamation of the gospel may impose a limit on future expansion? Is there not a grave danger of circumscribing God's blessing by it? In the past there has been steady increase, with the result that the present demand necessitates a hall of these dimensions; but is that to be our measure for the future? Are we contemplating no further increase? Are we setting bounds to God? If we accept what He has done in the past as the measure of His future working, then His blessing in the past will become a hindrance to future blessing. We shall be faced with stagnation and shall be in a deplorable state.

It is twenty years since some of us set out to serve the Lord and we are just where we were a score of years ago. Some of us have been engaged in His service as many as thirty years, yet we are still where we were away back then. Oh! we must shake ourselves free from all trammels of the past. Even under the most trying circumstances we must be full of expectation. The greater our expectation, the greater the opportunity

God will have for His working. We must enlarge our hearts and enlarge our horizon so that He can have a free way to do what He desires. Never let us assess His ability to work by our own limited capacity. Four thousand can be fed and satisfied with a few loaves, and so can five thousand. It is the measure of blessing that determines the measure of nourishment provided for the hungry multitudes. If only the stream of blessing is full, there is no limit to the fruit that will be found wherever it flows. If in our gatherings together we—this group of the Lord's servants—had our expectation centred on His blessing, the fruitfulness of the work in coming days would surpass all our asking or thinking.

God's blessing can be compared to a bird that is flying outside the room and you are seeking to lure it inside. Try as you may, you cannot induce it to fly in. If of its own accord it should do so, then you will have to be on the alert lest it fly out again. You could not persuade it to enter, but you can easily cause it to depart. Just a little carelessness on your part, and it is gone! So in the matter of divine blessing. It is God Who takes the initiative; no effort is called for from our side; but when His blessing has been freely bestowed it takes only a little heedlessness on our part to lose it.

During the past two or three years I have seen this thing happen among us. One fellow-worker had a few words with another fellow-worker. What he said was perfectly right, and what he did was right too; but I kept saying within myself: Brother, you're certainly right, but are we who serve the Lord merely governed by what is right? Is it right and wrong that determines our service for Him, or is it His blessing? Much that you have done may stand the test of right and wrong, but what if the divine blessing does not rest on those right things you have done? The question we need to ask in relation to all our activity is not, Am I right in doing this? but, Have I the blessing of the Lord on this? If we are to impose no restraint on His blessing, then we shall have to accept His restraint on our words and on all our conduct. It is so easy to forfeit God's blessing, and in forfeiting it yourself, to cause your fellow-worker to miss His blessing too. Yes, what you have done may be quite right, but you do not need to have done wrong to lose the divine favour.

God's blessing can never abide on what is wrong, but it cannot always abide on what is right. It is invariably found where brethren are living in harmony, but never where there is discord among them. Do realise that it is a serious thing for you to be at variance with any brother, even if a consideration of every aspect of the case proves you to be right. Brethren, let me warn you solemnly to give heed to your words. At all costs avoid criticism lest you forfeit the favour of the Lord and the work suffer in consequence. Divine work is not built up by human power or human gifts; it is built up by the divine blessing. If we lose that we lose everything.

What do we mean when we talk of God's blessing? We mean divine activity that is not based on human activity. We mean a working of God that is not based on our work. The blessing of God is not something we can earn by our efforts. It is not something we can buy with our money. One penny should always procure one pennyworth; but if without our one penny God gives us ten thousand pennyworth, that is His blessing. His blessing makes all our calculations futile because it leaves us without any basis on which to calculate. When five small loaves provide nourishment for five thousand people and leave a surplus that fills twelve baskets that is God's blessing!

We assess a person at a certain rate, and according to our assessment there should be certain results from his work. But results do not tally with our reckoning. We consider a certain worker to be illequipped for the work, but his ministry is very fruitful. The fruit is altogether out of proportion to his resources. How does this come about? It is because fruitfulness in the Lord's work is in proportion to His blessing, not in proportion to our limited gifts and limited power. Or, to go even further, His blessing brings a measure of fruitfulness that our failures and our frailty would never allow us to expect.

If our expectation is not based on what we are in ourselves, but solely on the blessing of the Lord, we shall see fruit in the work beyond all our ability to conceive. Are we full of hope regarding the future of the work, or are we full of our own calculations? Many brothers and sisters reckon with no more result than their own meagre measure would warrant their expecting. But the blessing of the Lord brings us into a realm where all reasonings are ruled out, for fruitfulness in the work is out of all proportion to what the worker has or is. In human affairs we reason from cause to effect, but all our reasonings are irrelevant in the realm of divine blessing, for in that realm God is the Cause, He alone.

Let us then cease to base our expectation on our resources lest we forfeit His grace. He cannot do the unexpected for us while we are expecting results in proportion to our own arduous efforts. We must place ourselves within the sphere of His blessing and say to Him: "Lord, for Thy name's sake, for Thy Church's sake, for the sake of making a way for Thee, we trust Thee to bless us beyond all our deserts." This is the kind of faith that avails in His service. It is trusting Him to work out of all correspondence to what we might reasonably expect. This faith is not based on any relation between cause and effect in the human realm, but is based on the effect of God's blessing of which He is the sole Cause. Provided our expectation is in Him alone, I believe we shall see the effects of His blessing on all our future way.

At times it seems that God not only grants no blessing, but even deliberately withholds it. For God to withhold His blessing is a very different thing from not adding His blessing. It is a most serious thing. There are times when the power released and the gifts exercised in the work warrant our expecting certain results; but the expected results are lacking. "We toiled all night and took nothing"—that is our experience. And that surely is less than we should reasonably expect. But why this vain toil? God has withheld His blessing.

I wonder if you feel the force of this. It is useless to argue here. The question is not how much your have toiled. The question is not whether you have done well or ill. The fact that has to be faced is this—God's blessing has not rested on your work. To think it is possible to toil all night and all our toil go unblessed! The object of our being on the earth is not that we may do right things, but that we may be vessels for the divine blessing. David made serious mistakes: Abraham was not without his mistakes either: Isaac was not a person of much account in himself: as for Jacob, he was a schemer; but the blessing of God rested on each one of these lives. Perhaps we who are gathered here today compare favourably with Jacob; but what does it amount to if the Lord does not bless us? Oh, that we might be those upon whom His blessing can abide! With that, numbers of souls will be saved and the work will expand far beyond its present bounds; without that, the unsaved will not be brought to the Lord and the saved will not be built up, so they will be reluctant to offer themselves and their all to Him and to go forth to other parts for His name's sake.

We are in urgent need of the Lord's blessing. Granted that one thing, little else will matter. As we have previously pointed out, even if in the past we have made mistakes that we thought must seriously prejudice our future work, they will be of little moment where the tide of divine blessing flows. The wrong hymn may be chosen at a meeting, but if the blessing of the Lord is on the meeting, there will be fruit from that wrong hymn. A message may be given that seems unsuited to the audience, but the audience will be blessed. Another group of people may gather, and another inappropriate message be given, but again the message will be blessed, and the need of this company will be met as was the need of the other. Do not misunderstand me, I am not suggesting that it does not matter if we do our work carelessly; but I am seeking to stress the fact that where the blessing of the Lord flows freely it sweeps away all that would impede its course. Nothing can stand before it. God said: "Jacob I loved, but Esau I hated." His good pleasure was toward Jacob, so His blessing rested on Jacob's life. Never let us lightly esteem the blessing of the Lord. It will issue in the salvation of souls and in the consecration of lives and possessions. The blessing of the Lord resting on one life may mean the salvation of fifty lives; it may mean the consecration of a hundred lives. God's blessing has momentous results.

But let us not forget that the flow of God's blessing can be hindered by us. Just a few critical words, just a wrong attitude, just a personal opinion—and the blessing is gone! May we be stabbed wide awake to the grave possibility of arresting it. To do that is to commit a heinous sin, for we may thereby endanger hundreds or even thousands of souls. May God be gracious to us so that we shall be those who expect His blessing and who, having received it, do not lose it again.

Brethren, let us learn henceforth to live in the blessing of the Lord. Let this vast sphere become our habitat. In all our work and in all our conduct may we be kept abiding here. Unless this becomes our settled sphere of life we shall suffer serious loss. One day in the year 1945, when Brother Lee was in Shanghai, he remarked that God's blessing was manifestly on our gatherings. Our brother has seen something here, and it is essential that we all come to the point where the one thing we are looking for in connection with the work is the divine blessing upon it. Much undreamt-of development will take place then.

We should always be expecting to see God work miracles. It should become natural to us to expect the supernatural. We must no longer look for results that are just in keeping with our capacity. We must cease to limit God by our limited measure. I repeat yet again, that unless we come to the place where we reckon with His blessing, there is little hope for the future. There is no prospect ahead unless we give up depending on our own hard earnings to maintain the work. If we have to accumulate sufficient wages to buy bread for the needy multitudes, years and years will elapse before their need is met. We must expect God to work beyond all that man can conceive. May God give us a vision of His blessing!

To be a person on whom the blessing of God can abide is of far more value than to be richly endowed with power and gifts; but, as we have said before, not everyone lives in the flow of His blessing. You may have a more congenial disposition than your brother and be more gifted than he; but for all that, his spiritual effectiveness surpasses yours. You may despise others and consider yourself superior to them; but do you think God is arbitrary in bestowing His blessing on them and not on you? You need to learn that the reason for your ineffective ministry lies in your own life. You have not provided God with the ground on which His blessing can rest.

These considerations should cause us to cease from our petulance and jealousies, and should lead us to judge ourselves unsparingly. You may be able to produce sound reasons for your justification, but what have you gained if God's blessing is withheld? Even if you should be proved right, what does it amount to if souls are not saved? And if you be proved better than others, what gain is that if the Church is not built up? All your rightness avails nothing.

From this day on let us avoid all questions of right and wrong and be those upon whom God's blessing can rest in abundant measure.

CHAPTER FIVE

GOD'S PURPOSE AND GOD'S REST

GOD'S PURPOSE

What was the purpose of God in the creation of man? God Himself has told us in Genesis chapter one. There we see that man was a distinctive creation. Before his creation God said: "Let us make man in our image, after our likeness: and let them have dominion over the fish of the sea, and over the fowl of the air, and over the cattle, and over all the earth, and over every creeping thing that creepeth upon the earth" (verse 26). This was God's design. God then proceeded to create man according to His design—"And God created man in his own image, in the image of God created he him; male and female created he them. And God blessed them: and God said unto them, Be fruitful, and multiply, and replenish the earth, and subdue it; and have dominion over the fish of the sea, and over the fowl of the air, and over every living thing that moveth upon the earth" (27, 28).

God wanted a man: God wanted a man to have dominion: God wanted a man to have dominion on the earth.

And God wanted man to be like Himself.   This clearly shows that man has a unique place in the creation. Of all created things man alone was made in the image of God.   The man of God's desire was to be totally different from every other created thing.

God sought to meet His own need through man. His creation called for someone to exercise control, and God chose man to be that one.   God wanted man to govern, and He wanted man to govern in a specific realm—"upon the earth."   The earth was to be the sphere of man's dominion. "And God said unto them... replenish the earth, and subdue it; and have dominion... upon the earth."

But man sinned and came under the dominion of Satan.   It seemed then as though all was at an end. Apparently Satan had triumphed and God had been defeated.

Psalm 8

Psalm 8 shows that the purpose of God is unchanging.   After the Fall God's will for man and His requirements of man remained as they had been before the Fall.   Though man had fallen, the Psalmist could still sing his song of praise, because he had not lost sight of Genesis 1.   And God had not forgotten Genesis 1.   Let us look at the content of this psalm.

"O Lord, our Lord, How excellent is thy name in all the earth!" (verse 1).   Despite the fact that some men were blaspheming the name of the Lord and others

were rejecting His name, the Psalmist cries aloud:
"How excellent is thy name in all the earth!" He does
not say, "Thy name is excellent," as though he could
express its worth; he says in effect—Though I am a
poet, I cannot utter its worth, I can only say, "How
excellent!" And it is not only inexpressibly excellent,
it is so "in all the earth." That corresponds to Genesis
1. If we saw the purpose of God our hearts would be
stirred every time we read the word "man" and every
time we read the word "earth".

The second verse reads: "Out of the mouth of
babes and sucklings hast thou established strength,
because of thine adversaries, that thou mightest still the
enemy and the avenger." The Lord Jesus quotes the
verse thus: "Out of the mouth of babes and sucklings
thou hast perfected praise" (Matt. 21.16). Even if the
enemy should do his worst God need not deal with him;
a praising people can "still the enemy."

Verses 3-6 read: "When I consider thy heavens,
the work of thy fingers, The moon and the stars, which
thou hast ordained; What is man, that thou art mindful
of him? And the son of man, that thou visitest him?
For thou hast made him but little lower than the angels,
and crownest him with glory and honour. Thou madest
him to have dominion over, the work of thy hands;
Thou hast put all things under his feet." If we had been
writing the psalm we should probably have added a
parenthesis such as this—(Alas! man fell: he sinned

and had to be driven out of the garden of Eden, so he failed to reach the goal.) But, thank God! there was no such thought in the heart of the psalmist. So he tells the old story, completely ignoring the interlude of Genesis 3. That is the distinctive feature of Psalm 8.

The last verse reads like the first: "O Lord, our Lord, How excellent is thy name in all the earth!" The Psalmist concludes his song as though he had not so much as noted the fall of man. Adam could sin and Eve could sin: but Adam's sin and Eve's sin could not reverse the will of God. God's purpose for man was as it had ever been. Oh, God is eternally the same! There is no deviation in His ways: they go straight forward.

Hebrews 2

Genesis 1 speaks of God's will at the time of the creation of man: Psalm 8 speaks of God's will after the fall of man: Hebrews 2 speaks of God's will in the redemption of man. Let us now look at Hebrews 2.

"For not unto angels did he subject the world to come whereof we speak. But one hath somewhere testified, saying, What is man, that thou art mindful of him? Or the son of man, that thou visitest him? Thou madest him a little lower than the angels; thou crownedst him with glory and honour, And didst set him over the work of thy hands: thou didst put all things in subjection under his feet" (5-8a). That was as God originally intended. "But now we see not yet all things subjected to him. But we behold him who hath been made a little lower than the angels, even Jesus, because of the suffering of death crowned with glory and honour." In Psalm 8 it says that God made man a little lower than the angels, whereas here the writer substitutes "Jesus" for "man", i.e., he interprets the term "man" as applying to Jesus. It is at this point that redemption comes in. The passage continues: "that by the grace of God he should taste death for every man." God's original intention was that man should have dominion. The Lord Jesus is that Man. Hallelujah! that Man has already overthrown the power of Satan. In that Man God's desire is realised. And that Man is related to us.

"For it became him, for whom are all things, and through whom are all things, in bringing many sons unto glory, to make the author of their salvation perfect through sufferings" (verse 10). Thank God! His purpose has not altered. As it was at the time of creation, so it was still after man's fall, and so it remains in the day of redemption. God still intends to secure a company of men after the image of His Son. As He is, so they too will be: and as He has entered into the glory, so also will they.

But how can such a thing be? "For both he that sanctifieth and they that are sanctified are all of one" (verse 11). Who is "he that sanctifieth"? The Lord Jesus. And who are "they that are sanctified"? We!

We might read the sentence thus: "The Lord Jesus
Who sanctifies, and we who are sanctified, are all of
one." The Lord Jesus, and we who have been sanctified
by Him, have proceeded from the one Source: we are
partakers of the one Life: we are indwelt by the one
Spirit: one God is His Father and our Father, "for which
cause he is not ashamed to call them brethren" (11b).

GOD'S REST

Rest comes after work. And rest is only possible
when the work is accomplished, and when it is accomplished to a point of satisfaction. If a piece of work
is not completely finished, or if it does not meet with
approval, there is no possibility of rest.

Let us not think it was a small matter that God
rested after those six days of creation. Something must
have been secured for Him to be able to rest. It must
have taken a tremendous power to cause God—this
God of purpose, this God of abounding life—to come
to rest. How could He? Gen. 1.31 gives the reason.
"God saw everything that he had made, and, behold,
it was very good."

God rested on the seventh day. Before the seventh
day He worked. And before He set to work He had
an objective. Ephesians refers to it as "the mystery of
his will," "his good pleasure," "what he foreordained.".
God is not only a God of action, He is a God of purpose.
He does things because He wants to do them. His

outward acts are the result of inward desire. God came
to rest because He had done things to His satisfaction.
If we want to understand God's heart desire, His plan,
His good pleasure, we only need to see what it was that
could cause Him to rest. If we see God coming into
rest in relation to anything, then we know that thing
was what He was after originally. No man can rest
in relation to what does not satisfy him. Man must
have what he wants before he can rest. This matter
of rest is of great significance. Throughout the six days
God could not rest. Rest did not come till the seventh
day. He could rest then because He had accomplished
the thing that was dear to His heart. God's rest
proclaimed His approval: it proclaimed the attainment
of His goal: it proclaimed that His good pleasure was
realised to a point beyond which there could be no
fuller realisation. God is a God Who must be satisfied.
And God is a God Who can secure His satisfaction.
He has secured what He wanted, therefore He has
entered into rest.

But what was it that caused God to find rest?
What was it that provided His satisfaction? Let us
read Gen. 1.27-28 once again: "And God created man
in his own image, in the image of God created he him;
male and female created he them. And God blessed
them: and God said unto them, Be fruitful and
multiply, and replenish the earth, and subdue it; and
have dominion over the fish of the sea, and over the

fowl of the air, and over every living thing that moveth upon the earth." Then follow these words: "And God saw everything that he had made, and, behold, it was very good" (verse 31). "And God blessed the seventh day and hallowed it: because that in it he rested from all his work which God had created and made" (Gen. 2.3).

God's purpose was to have a man: to have a man who could exercise dominion: to have a man who could exercise dominion on the earth. On the sixth day of the creation God's purpose was attained; therefore on the seventh day "he rested from all his work."

CHAPTER SIX

SPECIAL GRACE AND RESERVE GRACE

Question:— What is the cause of poverty in the life of a Christian?

Answer:— In Rev. 3 the Lord said, "I know ... thou art ... poor." These words were addressed by Him to the church in Laodicea. The poverty here referred to implied that nothing had been laid up in store. It implied not merely a momentary lack, but a continuous lack.

A FUNDAMENTAL DIFFICULTY

Many Christians eke out a hand-to-mouth existence. This is a serious problem. They are dependent on temporary supplies of grace; they have no permanent supply. God's work in our lives is wholly a work of grace, and if He removed His grace from us our lives would be an utter void. This is a fact which we need to recognise. Nevertheless, it is also a fact that God's grace should be ever increasingly stored up in our lives; otherwise we shall be dependent on special gracious interventions in order to be kept in His will. It is not well-pleasing to Him if His children live from hand to mouth. He desires us to have a rich store of grace in our lives.

Many people have no such store, and for that reason the Lord has told us to fast and pray. When on a certain occasion the disciples asked Him why they were unable to cast out the demon that tormented a child, He told them that their impotence could only be overcome by prayer and fasting. Unless we discipline ourselves strictly we shall become dependent on special dispensations of grace. If we have just newly come to the Lord that is not an abnormal condition; but if after we have been His for a year or two we are still dependent on such experiences it indicates a state of poverty and sickness.

WHAT IS WEALTH?

Wealth is the reverse of poverty. To be spiritually wealthy is to have a reserve of grace. There is no poverty in a life in which the grace of God has been stored up over the years. Poverty is banished by an overplus of grace.

The other day a few of us talked together about Paul's epistles to the Corinthians. For my part I believe that in those epistles more than anywhere else in the entire New Testament we get a revelation of the life of a Christian. Here the man, Paul, is set before us. In his letter to the Romans he unfolds the depths of saving grace, and in his letter to the Ephesians he brings forth the profoundest revelation; but when he writes to the Corinthians we are able to make his personal acquaintance, for he opens up his heart and speaks intimately about himself.

Many people cannot minister the Word of God apart from special revelation. If at any given time they have no fresh revelation then their ministry comes to a standstill, because revelation is the source of all their utterance. That we need revelation if we are to have uttered ministry is a fact; but please bear this fact also in mind that revelation is not given us in unbroken continuity. It was not so in the case of the twelve apostles. And it was not so even in the case of such a man as Paul. In a certain instance he himself said, "I have no commandment of the Lord," yet despite that fact he continued to minister. He dared to utter what he himself believed without having any fresh word from the Lord. This is an amazing thing. He himself explains the ground on which he dared to minister at that time:– "I give my judgment as one that hath obtained mercy of the Lord to be faithful." Paul distinctly says that he was expressing his own judgment. He was not uttering what had been given him at that specific time, but was simply giving his own opinion on the matter which was then brought before him. What a terrific thing to do! Over the centuries theologians have questioned these utterances of Paul's, but Paul knew what he was saying. He dared at times to express himself on spiritual matters without immediate revelation. To speak under such circumstances would have been presumption on the part of others, but there was no presumption on Paul's part. Christians who have only received grace enough to meet the immediate need have to refrain from utterance till they receive some definite word from the Lord. But in Paul's case it was not so. The secret is this, that over the years there had been a ceaseless increase of the grace of God in his life.

In Paul we meet a man who affirms, and repeatedly affirms, that he has received no commandment from the Lord to speak (1 Cor. 7.6, 12, 25), and still he speaks. And finally, when he has said all he has to say on the matter under consideration, he still states that he is expressing his own judgment. But he concludes with this remark, "I think that I also have the Spirit of God" (I Cor. 7.40).

The most precious thing here is that though Paul was not consciously speaking the Word of God, he was all the while under the control of the Holy Spirit and was spontaneously expressing the mind of God. Some Christians are so ready to affirm that the Spirit is moving them to say this or that. They are so conscious that what they are uttering is God's Word. I fear such Christians betray their poverty. A wealthy Christian, out of the abundance of grace in his life, can speak the mind of God without the overweening consciousness of being God's mouthpiece. A wealthy Christian does not necessarily wait for something new and then, aware of having received it, speak as an oracle. But a Christian who has amassed no wealth over the years is afraid of speaking without the consciousness that what he is uttering has come to him then and there from God.

A FUNDAMENTAL PRINCIPLE

Paul was a man who had divine revelation, but when we meet him we touch something in a human life that was not imparted by revelation alone. For years he had followed the Lord, and for years he had not given way to sin nor even countenanced defeat; and over all those years his spiritual wealth was being continuously increased. So in course of time it came to pass that when he was faced with a need he could immediately speak the word that met the need. What an unveiling we get of the spiritual development of a human life as Paul opens his heart in the letters to the Corinthians! He tells us that he is only expressing his own judgment without specific revelation from the Lord, and yet we discover that what he has uttered is actually divine revelation to the Church. Here is a man who is speaking his own words and they are recorded in the Bible as the Word of God. Here we see the lofty heights to which, under the new covenant, the grace of God can bring a man. Here is a human life that has been wrought upon by God over the years. God has been ceaselessly moulding this life and purifying it till at length something has been wrought into the man's very constitution.

This is wealth. And this is the result of unremitting divine activity in a human life over long years of time. This did not come about by gifts of special grace on special occasions.

It is a great grief to me that I frequently meet brothers and sisters who are so dependent on special spiritual experiences that between the periodic help such experiences bring they lapse into a life like that of a non-Christian. What a poverty-stricken state this reveals! I acknowledge that if God's grace were removed from us we should all be utterly destitute; but while that is true, it is also true that there is a ceaseless operation of His grace which, if responded to, works something into our very being. Apart from inwrought grace in the life you will give way under trial. If you are spiritually poor you are found out when your prayers seem to go unheeded, when the heavens above are as brass and when everything seems to prove that God has forsaken you; and though you can get a temporary lift from church gatherings or other means of grace, you live a life of defeat in between such seasons. If, on the other hand, you have day by day gathered a store of wealth over the years, you are sustained under trial, however protracted.

Question:— How can we become wealthy?

Answer:— This is a question of fundamental importance.

    (1) Time is an essential Factor.

Permit me to say a very straight word to you younger brothers. You may think you are already rich, but none of you are really wealthy. Formerly we were of the opinion that some of the young people were ahead of the older ones spiritually; but recently in Foochow when we touched on deeper matters we discovered that many of the finest young folk had little experimental knowledge. May I appeal to you younger fellow-workers to remember that as yet you have not laid in store any great riches? Do not therefore be proud. To be proud is sheerest folly. You must realise that a long stretch of road has still to be covered before you reach that goal. And the goal will only be reached as you allow the Holy Spirit day by day to perform a work in your lives that will reconstitute and establish you. Time is a matter of primary importance here.

    (2) Trials are an essential Factor

There are many people who, despite the passage of years, have accumulated no riches because they have not passed through trials under the government of the Holy Spirit. Some Christians can go on day by day for years on end without coming in any definite way under the Spirit's control. They seem to go through life so easily. But other Christians are taken in hand and not let off, and all their circumstances are strongly governed by the Spirit of God. Some Christians gain little with the passage of time because they meet comparatively few difficulties. Even though there has been sufficient lapse of time to learn spiritual lessons, there has not been sufficient discipline in the life to produce spiritual wealth. Let us prize every circumstance into which are brought, and let us not be dismayed by whatever difficulties we meet for they are all ordered for our enrichment. The more trouble we encounter the more opportunity there is for spiritual increase in the life; and only thus shall we be able to bring the Word of Life to others. Wealth of ministry in the Word will be in proportion to the trials through which we have passed. We can only dispense to the children of God what we have gained by experience. We can only impart to them what we have actually learned from God Himself. This can never be acquired through doctrinal knowledge; but it can be acquired as we are led by the Holy Spirit through circumstances divinely ordered for our instruction.

Therefore I hope that we who are learning to follow the Lord will not be slack in our daily life. In all the disappointments and disillusionments we meet let us recognise the Lord's dealings with us and bow before Him in gratitude and worship, acknowledging that His purpose in all these things is to enrich our lives.

A certain brother thought himself to be quite strong

in faith till he fell ill. That trial disclosed to him how weak his faith was, but in the acceptance of the trial he began to learn what it really means to trust the Lord. Unless we meet difficulties we do not discover our need and do not learn simple dependence on Him and simple obedience to Him. Each time you meet a new difficulty just bow before the Lord and thank Him for the preciousness of the opportunity to learn something more of Him. Every outward frustration is an opportunity for inward gain. And as you receive all these God-given opportunities His grace will abound more and more toward you till you have a wealth of ministry for His Church. Oh, do not be deceived into thinking that by dint of much study you will be able to minister the Word richly. You may enrich your utterance thereby; but wealth of words can never be a substitute for spiritual wealth, and spiritual wealth can never be acquired from books. Much study may add to your intellectual knowledge and you can think you are rich, but your very wealth of words will betray your poverty of spirit. Spiritual wealth comes only in God's appointed way. We must pass through much suffering to gain it.

(3) Finality is an essential Factor.

It is not only essential that we pass through many trials over many days, it is equally essential that there be a clear issue in our lives. We must come through our trials to a place of finality. The Bible makes it abundantly plain that God deals with a life and will not let it go till He has brought it through to an issue. In His dealings with Job He allowed all his oxen and asses to be carried off, but that did not bring Job through to God's goal. Thereafter the sheep and the shepherds were all consumed by fire, and Job was still not through; nor even when all his sons and daughters died. He did not even emerge from his trials when he was covered with "sore boils from the sole of his foot unto his crown." But a day came when his lips were silenced in utter subjection to God, and Job's trials issued in a final triumph. James in his epistle refers to this as "the end of the Lord." Here we see that the question is not one of the number of our trials, but of the Lord reaching His end through them.

There is a solemn fact to be borne in mind here. We cannot pass through limitless trials. There is the possibility of wasted time and wasted suffering while God seeks to gain His end in our lives. It is tragically possible that all His dealings with us will fail to secure a vessel suited to His use. The clay may be moulded and remoulded in the Potter's hands and may pass through the fire again and again; and in the end there may be nothing but useless fragments. But our hope is that the time factor being provided by God, and the trials being appointed by Him, the issue will be "a vessel unto honour, sanctified, meet for the master's use."

Job not only passed through many trials, but a day

came when there was a new activity of God in his life, and that divine activity wrought a fundamental change in the man. God's object in all His dealings with us is not merely to dispense His life to us to meet the emergency of the hour; He wants to remake us by His indwelling life. It is a fact that the old creation cannot be changed and has therefore been consigned to the Cross, and it is also a fact that we now have the new creation life within us. But this further fact is taught by the Word of God that, by putting this new life within man, God has made it possible for man to be transformed. Man can be changed, changed constitutionally. There is a difference between Christian and non-Christian not only in this respect that the Christian possesses the divine life and the non-Christian does not, but in this further respect that, because of the activity of the divine life within the Christian his very being is altered. A change takes place when one human being lives for a time with another human being. Since that is so, it would be an astonishing thing for anyone to live with God and no change to take place in his life with the passing of time.

It is this fundamental change that we long to see in all who have received the divine life. We hope that day by day through the indwelling Spirit of God a ceaseless transformation will be taking place so that we may become of use to Him and have something to impart to others. We are not just looking for increased knowledge of the Word of God. And now that we have considered the life of Paul, we trust we shall not only know more about Paul, but that like him we shall learn to follow the Lord Himself and shall thus be enabled to serve Him and to serve others by ministering His Word to them.

And now, finally, let us consider the matter of inward illumination. A Christian who is spiritually rich is one who is greatly enlightened in spirit. What has been learned day by day over a period of time has taken clear shape in the life and can be expressed in words that bring enrichment to other lives. It is in this way that we become competent ministers of the Word of God. Often when we are under His hand we are too bewildered to understand what is happening to us, but when He has brought His dealings with us to an issue there is inward clarity. By the acceptance of His dealings with us we have been matured in faith and obedience, and so that needful thing has taken place in our lives of which Rev. 3 speaks:— "I counsel thee to buy of me eye-salve that thou mayest see."

Question:— Is this enlightenment of which you speak different from revelation?

Answer:— Yes, it is different. This light comes through revelation, but it is not just external light, it is inward light. What hinders the breaking of light within is failure to obey.

Question:— Swift obedience is a matter of receiving

swiftly from the hands of the Lord whatever He sends, is it not?

Answer:— Yes, that is true. But here I think it is
necessary for us to understand the government of the Holy Spirit.

The Holy Spirit not only operates in the believer
making His demands within the life; He operates in
outward circumstances too, suiting the circumstances of
the believer to the goal He has in view. Even if there
be resistance in the life, the Spirit of God will order
circumstances in such a way as to attain His own goal
in the life, and by His sovereign ordering of circumstances will bring that life to unswerving obedience.
He will work until a point is reached in the life when,
without any determination on the part of the believer
to obey, he instinctively obeys. If some of you who have
been the Lord's for a long time cast a glance over your
past history, you will be able to recall occasions when
He spoke and you obeyed instantly. But you can recall
other occasions when He spoke and you failed to
respond; yet strangely, after a time you just found yourself in a way of obedience. At certain times you may
have put up a resistance to the Lord's will and may have
persisted in this resistance; then somehow—quite unac-
countably—you found the resistance had gone. Such
is the fruit of the Holy Spirit's government of our lives.
Praise God, if His Spirit is handling these lives of ours,
even if we seem totally unable to obey and cannot even

exercise faith, a day comes when the resistance has vanished and we are trusting the Lord in simplicity of heart. It is the tireless energy of the Holy Spirit that has accomplished this. He has resource to work in us the obedience we lack.

There are two aspects of the Spirit's government. The one is, to order our affairs in such a way that through His circumstantial dealings with us we come to a point where we offer our willing obedience. The other is that, even when we have no intention to obey, His activity in our lives makes good what we lack so that, despite our unwillingness, we become obedient.

A certain brother was bound by the love of money. The Spirit of God dealt with him again and again, but he only chafed under the trials that befell him and gripped his money as tightly as ever. But the fact is, his love of money is gone. How this happened even he himself does not know. One day he asked me: "Which do you think is better, to be obedient and lose your love of money, or to be disobedient and lose it? I answered, "That money has lost its attraction for you is the thing that matters. How that came about is of little account." Nevertheless, let us seek grace of God to be swiftly obedient. That will obviate needless chastisement and bring us speedily through. In either case, the activity of the Holy Spirit is exceedingly precious.

Question:— How can we obey swiftly?

Answer:— When the Holy Spirit of God moves within us, obedience is instant; when He works by outword means it takes time to achieve His end. In the latter case He deals with the unwillingness that hinders His work till the necessary inner change takes place and resistance gives way.

How can we, being what we are, ever reach God's goal? How can we ever attain so lofty a standard as that set before us in chapters 4 and 5 of the Ephesian epistle? What hope is there that we shall ever "attain unto the unity of the faith and of the knowledge of the Son of God, unto a fullgrown man, unto the measure of the stature of the fulness of Christ"? What hope is there that the Church will ever become "a glorious church, not having spot or wrinkle or any such thing"? There is this hope—the Holy Spirit is ceaselessly active to bring us to God's goal, and He is not only moving within the life of the believer, He is ordering the outward affairs of the believer making all conducive to the one end.

The government of the Holy Spirit is a great reality. There are many things in our lives that militate against the purpose of God, some of which we seem totally unable to throw off; and yet a day comes when we find they are gone. The providential ordering of our ways has brought this about. What a gospel this is! What a marvellous thing it is that the Christian can reckon

with the government of God's Holy Spirit to make
good what he lacks!

CHAPTER SEVEN

GOD'S KEEPING POWER

Scripture Reading: Num. 13.25-33; 14.4-10; Josh. 14.6-12.

It is a distressing fact that some Christians can believe in God's saving power, but they cannot believe in His keeping power. They do not realise that He Who is the Giver of grace is also the One Who maintains us in His grace. Let us see from the Scriptures how we who have been saved by God can be kept by Him.

In Josh. 14.11 Caleb says: "I am as strong this day as in the day that Moses sent me: as my strength was then, even so is my strength now, for war, and to go out and to come in." "To go out and to come in" refers to everyday life: "for war" refers to life under exceptional circumstances. As Caleb's strength was in the day when Moses sent him to spy out the land of promise, so it was in the day when he uttered these words. He was able to cope with the ordinary demands of daily life and also with the demands of life under conditions of special stress. Though forty years had elapsed in the interval, he was as strong as he had been in his earlier days. Here we see God's keeping power.

As Caleb was in the prime of manhood, so he was in old age. He was no less vigorous at eighty-five than he had been at forty. There is only one explanation for this, he had been kept by God. We are totally unable to keep ourselves in the grace of God. There is no guarantee that even five years after we have been saved we shall be found in the measure of faith which we had in our earlier Christian life. We cannot by our own effort abide in the grace of God; it is He alone Who can maintain us in His grace.

How did Caleb come to experience God's keeping power? Josh.14.4 answers the question. "Because that he wholly followed the Lord, the God of Israel." And how did he wholly follow the Lord? We are told in Numbers 13 and 14. After the ten spies had brought back an evil report of the promised land, "Caleb stilled the people before Moses and said, Let us go up at once and possess it; for we are well able to overcome it." "We are well able to overcome" is the declaration of a person who wholly follows the Lord. He believes that victory over every foe is assured because the promises of God are trustworthy and because the Lord is with His people. Brothers and Sisters, do you believe? Many people believe, but their faith is a vascillating faith. They sing their song of praise, but though the words are right there is something wrong with the tune. In Caleb's case it was otherwise. He sang the right words in the right tune. Listen to the clear notes:

"Let us go up at once and possess it; for we are well able to overcome." "Let us go up at once!" A person who wholly follows the Lord and reckons Him to be trustworthy is one who does the will of God and does it at once.

What about the ten spies? They looked at the inhabitants of the land and saw that they were "men of great stature" and their cities were "fenced and very great." They looked at themselves too, and in their own sight they were "as grass-hoppers." Their eyes were fixed on the difficulties that challenged their advance. And herein lies the reason why so many Christians fail to experience God's keeping power—difficulties fill their vision.

God does not want us to gaze at the mountains obstructing our path, He wants us to say to the mountains: "Remove hence!" (Matt.17.20). Many people are all the time thinking of their failures, and by so doing they pave the way for further failure. Defeat is certain if we are constantly contemplating defeat. If we keep thinking there is no way through, that thought blocks the way through. We are courageous only as we keep God's promises in view. Alas that so many of God's people lack the virile faith that characterised Caleb and concentrate their thoughts on the intensity of their sufferings and the insurmountable nature of their difficulties! But those who do not fear "the sons of Anak"—the giants that inhabit the land of promise—are "well able to overcome." Caleb was so unafraid of the Anakim that he actually requested Joshua to appoint as his portion in the land of promise the mountain in which they had their strong-hold (Josh. 14.12-15). He was not dismayed by the fact that they were "men of great stature," nor by the fact that their cities were "great and fenced," so he overcame them without any strain. The whole question in relation to overcoming is: Are you trusting in yourself, or are you trusting in the Lord? If you are relying on yourself then of course you have to consider whether the Anakim are strong or weak, and whether their cities are well fortified or not; but if your reliance is on God, then the question of human resources does not even arise. If you are trusting in God there is no ground for fear since victory is assured to all who put their trust in Him.

There is another noteworthy matter in connection with Caleb. He exhorted the whole congregation of the children of Israel, saying: "Rebel not against the Lord, neither fear ye the people of the land; for they are bread for us." He sought to show the children of Israel that in the land itself there were resources upon which they could draw in order to possess it. "The people of the land . . . are bread for us," he declared. What is bread? Bread is something you eat. Bread is something that brings increased strength. The inhabitants of the land were admittedly "men of great stature," but Caleb proclaimed that they were food for God's people. He not only honoured God's promises, he despised the difficulties that stood in the way of their realisation. And every true believer, like Caleb, honours God and lightly esteems all obstacles. But this leaves no room for pride, for only they who humble themselves before God are able to take their stand on His side.

Every time you meet a difficulty, every time you find yourself in an impossible situation, ask yourself this question: Am I going to starve here, or am I going to eat the food that is set before me? If you are relying on the Lord for victory and let His overcoming life be manifested in you, you will find fresh nourishment and increased vitality in accepting as "bread" those Anakim that are contesting your progress. Do bear in mind that people who do not eat well cannot grow into maturity. Many people take the Word of God as their meat and the doing of His will as their meat, but they reject the Anakim as unpalatable food. The more we eat such food the stronger we shall become. Caleb is a grand illustration of this. Because he accepted the Anakim as "bread" he was still full of vitality at the age of eighty-five. So many Anakim had been assimilated by him over the years that he had developed a constitution which showed no trace of age. So it is in the spiritual realm. Some brothers and sisters have met few difficulties, but they are spiritually feeble. The explanation is, they have not consumed enough Anakim. On the other hand there are those who have met and overcome difficulty after difficulty, temptation after temptation; and they are full of vigour. The reason is, they have fed well on Anakim. Every difficulty and every temptation Satan puts in our way is food for us. This is a divinely appointed means of spiritual progress. The sight of any great trouble strikes terror into the heart of those who do not believe God, but those who trust Him say: "Praise God, here is some more food!" All our trials, without exception, are bread for us, and as we accept one trial after the other, we are more and more richly nourished and the result is a continuous increase of strength.

Let us now look into the practical outworking of this. We must not forget that there is a condition attached to God's keeping power. If we do not trust Him He is unable to keep us. In order to know His keeping power we must believe wholeheartedly in His promises. If we are harbouring doubts about our ability to overcome, then we are discrediting His ability to keep us. Every morning when we rise we should say to Him: "I thank Thee for keeping me yesterday, and today Thou wilt still keep me. I do not know what temptations may befall me, and I do not know how I can overcome; but I believe Thou wilt keep me." 1Pet.1.5 makes it clear that God keeps those who have faith in Him. It reads: "who by the power of God are guarded through faith." It is not we who have to grapple with temptations and try to overcome them; it is the keeping power of God that will get us through, and we must believe in His ability to save us from giving way to sin. Provided we rely implicitly on Him, even when we are unexpectedly assailed by temptations an amazing thing happens. In a way we cannot account for something wards off "all the fiery darts of the evil one." It is "the shield of faith." It comes in between us and Satan, so that his fiery darts cannot reach us. Instead of hurting us they beat upon the shield of faith and rebound on Satan himself.

Paul said, "I am persuaded that He is able to guard that which I have committed unto Him against that day" (11 Tim. 1.12). The Lord was able to keep Paul; but Paul did something that enabled the Lord to keep him. Paul committed himself to the Lord. If you believe in Him, then you must commit yourself to Him. He can only keep what has been handed over to Him. Many people fail to experience the blessedness of His keeping power because they have never put themselves into His care. They have never said to Him: Lord, I hand myself over to Thee and commit to Thee the keeping of my life." Brothers and Sisters, have you placed yourselves in His hands? If you truly have, then you will be able to say with Paul, "I am persuaded that He is able to guard that which I have committed unto Him against that day."

If your life is truly in His hands then God will fulfil in you the promise "to guard you from stumbling and to set you before the presence of His glory without blemish in exceeding joy" (Jude v.24). We stumble if we strike against something in a moment when we are unconscious of any obstruction in the way. Praise God, His preserving grace operates beyond the realm of our consciousness. Brothers and Sisters, if you commit yourselves unreservedly into his care, you will marvel at the way you are kept even when you have been unaware of danger.

When temptation suddenly assails and love is required, you will find love welling up from within and flowing out spontaneously to meet the challenge. Or if a sudden temptation demands patience, without your giving it a moment's thought patience will rise up to meet the need. Praise God, as the life we receive from Adam expresses itself spontaneously, so also does the life we receive from Christ. We inherit our bad tempers from Adam and can get angry without the slightest effort of will. We inherit pride from Adam and we can be proud without any deliberate decision. In the selfsame way, all who have received the life of Christ, and have committed themselves into His keeping, can be meek without making up their minds to be meek and can be humble without any attempt to be humble. The same spontaneity of manifestation that characterises the life we have received from Adam also characterises the life we have received from Christ. His life expresses itself unconsciously and without effort on our part.

Provided we trust in His promises and commit ourselves utterly to Him, we shall be kept from this day to the day of His return, and kept without blemish. Thank God, the saving grace into which He has brought us today is worthy of our trust and will carry us triumphantly through every trial that lies ahead.

CHAPTER EIGHT

WORSHIPPING THE WAYS OF GOD

Scripture Reading: Gen. 24.26-27, 52-53; Ex. 4.30-31, 12.27, 34.5-9; Josh. 5.13-14; Jud. 7.15; I Sam. 1.27-28; II Sam. 12.18-20; Job 1.13-20.

If we truly intend to be worshippers of God, then a day must come in our history when we realise that merely to know Him as our Father and ourselves as His children is totally inadequate. We need to know God as God and ourselves as His bondservants. Not until this revelation breaks upon us can we worship Him in truth. Not until we meet God as God can we really bow before Him. Not till then do we realise that we are His subjects. It is this realisation that begets worship. But it does not end there. Such a seeing of God not only causes us to fall down before Him; it leads us to recognise and accept His ways. The Scriptures show us that only by revelation can we know God. They also show us that only as we are subject to Him do we begin to know His ways.

What are God's ways? His ways are His method of doing what He has decided to do. And in relation to us they are the dealings with us whereby He realises His purpose concerning us. His ways are higher than our ways and they leave no room for our choice. He deals with one person in this manner and with another person in that manner, doing always as He deems best. His ways are the manner in which He Himself for His own good pleasure accomplishes what He has willed to do.

Many people baulk at the fact that, prior to an unveiling of God to man, man is incapable of accepting God's ways. The natural man keeps asking: Why did God love Jacob and not Esau? We bear a grudge against Jacob and try to defend Esau. Esau we think was a good man, extremely good. It was Jacob who was bad, very bad. Jacob was a supplanter, a deceiver. Yet God says: "Jacob I loved, but Esau I hated." And still we go on asking, Why? why? To question why God loved Jacob and not Esau proves that we have not seen God. Those who have seen Him have no questions here. They simply say, God is God: God does what He does because He is Who He is. No one dare tell Him how He should act. "Who hath been His counsellor?"

God's ways are the expression of His choice. They are the manifestation of His desire. What He has determined to do He does in the way that will secure His end. Hence His providential dealings with men vary according to the purpose He has in view for each life.

As we have already pointed out, when anyone through revelation really comes to see that God is God and that man is man, he can do no other than bow down and worship. But please bear in mind that only to go thus far is to fall short of the mark. That is too abstract a position. It is necessary to go a step further. Having been brought to a point where we worship God, we want not only to adore Him, but also to adore His ways. We bow before Him in adoration for what He is in Himself, and we also accept with adoration all the way He chooses to lead us and all the things it pleases Him to bring into our lives.

Brothers and Sisters, it is an easy thing to worship God as we are gathered here. There is no cost attached to it. But let me repeat once more that when we have really seen who God is we fall before Him and acknowledge that all His ways with us are right ways; we worship Him because He has done all things well.

We must learn to walk step by step; and if we walk before God we shall learn to adore His ways. Spiritually our entire future hinges on the matter of our worshipful acceptance of all His dealings with us. We must come to a point where we worship Him for everything it pleases Him to give and for everything it pleases Him to take away. In order that we may learn something of His ways let us consider a few of the Old Testament saints who, as true worshippers, learned to worship Him and His ways.

WORSHIPPING GOD FOR A PROSPEROUS WAY

Our first illustration is to be found in Gen. 24. You recall the story. Abraham said to Eliezer, the servant to whom he had given charge of his entire household: "Go unto my country and to my kindred, and take a wife for my son Isaac." This was a formidable undertaking. Abraham was then living in Canaan, and to reach Mesopotamina involved crossing two rivers and a stretch of desert in between. It was a difficult and delicate matter to go to a strange place a great distance off and persuade a young woman to accept this offer of marriage. But Eliezer was looking to God. And though his commission seemed to be taking him to the ends of the earth, one verse of Scripture covers it all — "He arose and went to Mesopotamia, unto the city of Nahor." How amazingly simple it was!

Having reached the city for which he was bound, he prayed: "O Lord, the God of my master Abraham, send me, I pray thee, good speed this day, and shew kindness unto my master Abraham. Behold, I stand by the fountain of water; and the daughters of the men of the city come out to draw water: and let it come to pass, that the damsel to whom I shall say, Let down thy pitcher, I pray thee, that I may drink; and she shall say, Drink, and I will give thy camels drink also: let the same be she that thou hast appointed for thy servant Isaac; and thereby shall I know that thou hast shewed kindness unto my master" (verses 12-14). Abraham's servant had not even finished praying when Rebekah arrived at the well, and to a detail all transpired as he had requested. But what if this damsel were not of Abraham's family? As you know, the type here is of Christ and the Church, both of the one family of God. "He that sanctifieth and they who are sanctified are all of one." The damsel must be of the same stock as Isaac; she dare not be of another race. So Eliezer asks about her connections. Yes, she is of Abraham's kindred. As soon as he was assured on this point, he "bowed his head, and worshipped the Lord."

Do you see the ways of God? Oh, let me tell you, if only you will learn to recognise God in all His dealings with you, you will surely worship Him. If you request Him to do this and that and look trustfully to Him, and then things fall out as you asked, you will adore Him for His ways with you. When Eliezer saw things happen exactly as he had asked, "the man bowed his head and worshipped the Lord. And he said, Blessed be the Lord, the God of my master Abraham, who hath not forsaken His mercy and His truth toward my master: as for me, the Lord hath led me in the way to the house of my master's brethren."

Brothers and Sisters, do you see what it means to worship God? It is to render all glory to Him. When you are faced with some difficulty about which you have sought Him and are carried through, do you just rejoice in the prosperity of your way? It was not so with Abraham's servant. He did not even stop to talk to Rebekah, he straightway worshipped. He did not feel embarrassed: he did not halt for a moment's consideration: he instantly bowed his head and his lips uttered these words, "Blessed be the Lord!"

Have I made myself sufficiently clear? I long that you might see the connection between glory and worship. To bring glory to the Lord is to worship Him, and it is our bowing before Him that is true worship. The proud in heart cannot worship Him because they do not bow to Him. When their way is prosperous they attribute it to their own ability or to chance; they do not give the glory to God. To be a true worshipper is to offer praise and thanksgiving to Him for everything we meet. At every turn Abraham's servant did so. When he went with Rebekah to her home and explained his mission and he found Laban and Bethuel willing to let Rebekah go at once, he did not stop to think about his own prosperity, or the fortunate turn of events; he did not think of people or things. Again his instantaneous reaction was to adore the ways of God. "He bowed himself down to the earth unto the Lord."

Brothers and Sisters, we must learn to recognise God's ways. I do not know how to press this truth home, but I would iterate and reiterate it. We Christians need to know the will of God, but we also need to know His ways. We need to recognise His works, but we also need to recognise the way He works. We must learn to worship Him for what He is in Himself, but we must also learn with worshipping hearts to accept His ways of working. This was an outstanding characteristic in the life of Abraham's servant. His reaction to everything he met was to bow before God in adoration of His ways.

If our hearts are set to be worshippers of God He will give us more and more opportunity to worship Him. It was so with Eliezer. As the way opened up before him, at each new stage he saw a new opportunity. God orders all our affairs so that we may bring to Him the worship He desires. At times He makes our way so prosperous that we have to acknowledge it was He alone Who did it, and all the glory goes to Him.

WORSHIPPING GOD   FOR HIS CEASELESS CARE

Our second illustration is found in Ex.4. When God sent Moses and Aaron to tell the children of Israel that He had seen their affliction and was about to deliver them from the bondage of Egypt, "the people believed: and when they heard that the Lord had visited the children of Israel, and that He had seen their affliction, then they bowed their heads and worshipped."

Do you see this people worshipping God for His ways? Again and again God brings things to pass in our history so that we cannot but worship Him. This was true of Abraham's servant. But the situation recorded here is a very different one. No change had actually taken place in the condition of God's people when they bowed their heads in worship. They had only been assured that God had seen their affliction and was going to deliver them. They were told by Moses and Aaron that God had not forgotten them those four hundred and more years, but had seen all their sufferings. It was this assurance that provoked their worship.

We are often unable to worship God because in our trials we think He has forgotten us. We are cast down because of prolonged domestic difficulties; but whose domestic difficulties have lasted 430 years? We have been sick and have long hoped for healing: we have been out of employment for years and still cannot find a job: those who are closest to us refuse to believe in the Lord: the same old harrassing circumstances remain. So we come to the conclusion that God has not taken note of all our trials and has left us to our own resources. How can we worship Him? Our lips are silenced. But a day comes when we see God and understand His ways, and immediately we know that He has never forgotten us. In that day the silent lips are opened, and with bowed head we acknowledge that all that has befallen us has been working for our good. We see God's grace in everything and we adore His ways.

WORSHIPPING GOD FOR HIS SALVATION

In Ex.12,27 God instructed His people to answer

their children in this wise when they asked the meaning of the Passover — "It is the sacrifice of the Lord's passover, who passed over the houses of the children of Israel in Egypt, when he smote the Egyptians, and delivered our houses." How did His people receive this message from the Lord? "The people bowed the head and worshipped." Note that the Passover was essentially a memorial sacrifice. As such it invariably provoked worship. God destroyed the firstborn in all the houses of the Egyptians, but He passed over all the houses of the children of Israel. As they recalled the difference God had put between His people and the world, and the different destination for which they were bound, they could not but adore Him.

The Breaking of Bread, like the Passover, is a memorial feast, an occasion to recall God's mighty work in separating us from the world; and the recollection of it begets worship in our hearts. We wonder how it ever came about that He separated us from the world to Himself. We wonder at His ways and worship. When God's people of old saw that the whole land of Egypt was visited with destruction and not a single Egyptian home was spared, yet their homes were all passed over and not one of their firstborn perished, how could they but worship Him? And we who are not only recipients of His grace, but have been led to see the wondrous ways in which He has wrought in order to impart that grace to us, how can we but adore Him?

Has the manner of God's working in relation to your own life not come home to you? Have you not been arrested by the way in which He has moved, choosing you out from multitudes around you and making you His own? Oh, I think of it often. When I was saved I was a student. I had over 400 fellow-students, and out of all that number God's choice lighted on me. How did it come about? I was one of a large clan, and out of the whole clan God chose me. How did that happen? Oh, when we think of His grace in saving us we praise Him; but when we think of the marvellous ways by which His grace reached us we worship Him. It is the manner in which He has worked that overwhelms us so that our hearts are filled with wonder, and we fall down before Him in adoration and acknowledge that He is God, He alone.

Brothers and Sisters, you ask why He saved you. Let me tell you that He saved you because it was His delight to save you. He wanted to, and because He wanted to He chose you and brought you to Himself. So there is nothing for you to say, nothing for you to do, nothing but just to worship Him.

At the Breaking of Bread as you contemplate His grace in saving you, imparting His righteousness to you who were unrighteous, in bestowing His life to you that you might become His child, your heart goes out in thanksgiving to Him. But when you think of the way by which He accomplished this: when you think of the pains He took to draw you out of the miry pit: when you think how He brought you into just the right circumstances to prepare your heart so that at length you opened it to Him, you behold His ways and you adore Him.

There is a point to note in the verse we have been considering. When Moses told the children of Israel the meaning of the Passover "the people bowed the head and worshipped." Note that this act was not the result of any instruction from Moses. He did not tell them they ought to worship God. They simply did it. It was their spontaneous reaction when he mentioned the significance of the Passover. Worship is not the fruit of mental exercise; it is begotten by beholding the ways of God.

WORSHIPPING GOD AT THE PROCLAMATION OF HIS WAYS

In Ex.32-34 we read of a serious difficulty Moses encountered. Alone on the Mount with God the ten commandments, written on two tables of stone, were committed to him. Meanwhile trouble had broken out on the plain. The people had made a golden calf and worshipped it. This provoked God to great displeasure and He said to Moses: "Go, get thee down; for thy people, which thou broughtest up out of the land of Egypt, have corrupted themselves: they have turned aside

quickly out of the way which I commanded them: they
have made them a golden calf, and have worshipped it,
and have sacrificed unto it, and said, These be thy gods,
O Israel, which brought thee up out of the land of Egypt.
And the Lord said unto Moses, I have seen this people,
and, behold, it is a stiffnecked people: now therefore
let me alone, that my wrath may wax hot against them,
and that I may consume them: and I will make of thee
a great nation." When Moses saw that God's wrath
was stirred against His people he besought God for them,
then went down to deal with the situation on the plain.
Thereafter he ascended the Mount again and in obedience
to God's command hewed two tables of stone like the
first which he had broken, and with these in his hand
he went to the top of Mount Sinai where God made a
solemn proclamation, the first part of which was this:
"The Lord, the Lord, a God full of compassion and
gracious, slow to anger, and plenteous in mercy and
truth; keeping mercy for thousands, forgiving iniquity
and transgression and sin." If at that point Moses had
fallen down and worshipped God it would not have
been surprising; but it was after the second part of the
proclamation that he did so, and the second part was
totally different from the first. The earlier part spoke
of God's compassion, and grace, and mercy and forgiveness; but the latter part was this: "and that will by no
means clear the guilty; visiting the iniquity of the fathers
upon the children, and upon the children's children,

upon the third and upon the fourth generation." It was when God had proclaimed the awfulness of His majesty that "Moses made haste, and bowed his head to the earth, and worshipped." Please bear in mind that it is not merely grace that provokes worship. If we are to be worshippers of God we need to know His holiness.

I love verses 8 and 9 in chapter 34. In the latter verse Moses prays, but in the former he worships. He first worships, then prays. He first acknowledges the rightness of God's ways, then he seeks God's grace. He does not beseech God on the ground of His compassion, and grace, and plenteous mercy, and readiness to forgive, to reverse His decision. Our prayer would be like that. We are always trying to persuade God not to do what He has said He would do. Moses was very different from us. He took his right place before God and bowed to God's ways.

Brothers and Sisters, have you never asked God to do what you knew was contrary to His ways of working? Have you never besought Him to forgive a certain brother and cease to chasten him even when you knew that His dealings with that brother were right? That is not worshipping God. How often our prayers amount to requesting God to change His ways! Without considering His ways we just open our lips and ask Him to remove the pressure here, the sickness there and the domestic problems elsewhere. To pray after this fashion is seeking grace and ignoring the ways of God. We are making ourselves too big. We are not in our proper place before God. We are not bowing before Him. Moses was not like that. Before he prayed he first acknowledged God's sovereignty and accepted His ways. God had declared that He would "by no means clear the guilty; visiting the iniquity of the fathers upon the children, and upon the children's children, upon the third and upon the fourth generation." Moses instantly accepted God's proclamation of His ways and "bowed his head toward the earth and worshipped." He recognised this to be God's way of working, and he capitulated. Thereafter he prayed that, if he had found grace in God's sight, God would still go up in the midst of His people. He did pray for grace, but not until he had unreservedly accepted God's ways.

You visit a certain home and find a sick child there, and you pray with the parents for the healing of the child, though you are aware that God is not being glorified in the home; but because the parents plead with Him for healing you join in their request. To pray like that is asking God to change His ways. It is dictating to Him what He should do. You know God as Father and on that basis present your prayer; but let me repeat it once more that we need not only to know God as our Father, we need to know God as God.

You visit another home. Again there is a sick child in the home. And again you kneel in prayer with the parents. But these parents are praying like this: "Lord, we praise Thee for permitting this sickness. We worship Thee because Thou doest all things well. If it please Thee to take the child we accept Thy will; but if it please Thee to show mercy we ask Thee to heal him." To seek God's grace is right. The acceptance of God's ways does not rule out prayer nor eliminate grace. But there is an order here. We first capitulate to God, then we pray to Him. Prayer is the expression of my will: worship is the acceptance of God's will.

How we need to learn from Moses! God made His ways known to him, and when he saw the holiness and majesty of God, he fell down before Him. He did not reason with God about the consequences to himself or to the people if God visited their iniquity to the third and fourth generation. Oh, how we need to recognise and to love God's ways, however they may affect us! Moses had his desires, and it was a consuming desire with him to enter the land of Canaan; but God's proclamation of His ways to Moses dispelled every personal desire and bowed him to the ground in worship. Brothers and Sisters, we must not only learn to accept God's will and do His work; we must learn to love His ways and to find our pleasure in all He does for His own good pleasure.

WORSHIPPING GOD AS THE LORD
OF HOSTS

The book of Joshua opens with God's commission

to him to lead His people into the land of Canaan. What a weighty responsibility! God's aged servant Moses had died and Aaron had died too; now he, a young man, was faced with this stupendous task. What must he have felt like? If Moses, with all his years of experience, was unable to bring the people into the land, what hope was there for one so young as he? How would he be able to cope with the seven tribes that inhabited the land, all of them formidable foes? And how could he lead a people like the children of Israel, with their fear of death and their constant complaints? Faced with such a challenge, do you wonder that Joshua was all but overwhelmed? At that point he saw a vision. A Man with a drawn sword appeared before him. Not recognising the Man, he asked, "Art thou for us or for our adversaries?" (5.13). The Man answered with a clear "Nay." He was neither for the one side nor for the other. He had come for one purpose — "As captain of the host of the Lord am I now come." Praise God, this is His purpose! Praise God, this is the purpose of the Lord Jesus! He has not come to help us, nor to help our enemies, but to take His place as Captain of the Lord's host. If you belong to the Lord's host, then He is your Captain. The question here is not one of receiving help, but of accepting leadership. He has not come to offer assistance, but to demand subjection. How did Joshua react when he heard that this Man had come as Captain of the Lord's host?

"Joshua fell on his face to the earth and did worship."

Do you see the ways of God here? Not a thing God does is done with the object of assisting you or assisting those who are against you. God does not stand in the midst of the conflict giving a little help here or there. He is in command of the forces, and He requires our submission. In the face of so many foes, for God to help us would not answer the need. But for us to submit to Him will solve the whole problem.

The issue is one of submission to His leadership. When He is in command all is well. The trouble today among God's children is that so many of us want everything to circle around us and everything to serve our interests. God will not have it so. When the question of capitulation to Him is settled, all other questions vanish. You do not know God if you think He can occupy a subordinate position in the battle. It is His place to lead: it is your place to submit. When you are in your right place under His command you will know what it means to worship; and you will know what it means to have the drawn sword wielded on your behalf.

WORSHIPPING GOD FOR OPENING THE WAY

In the book of Judges there is a section that relates to Gideon. In chapter 7 we see him in a great dilemma and with no assurance regarding the issue. It was in this state of uncertainty that he ventured into the

Midianite camp. There he heard one of the Midianites saying to another: "Behold, I dreamed a dream, and, lo, a cake of barley bread tumbled into the camp of Midian, and came into the tent, and smote it that it fell, and turned it upside down, that the tent lay along. And his fellow answered and said, This is nothing else save the sword of Gideon the son of Joash, a man of Israel: into his hand God hath delivered Midian and all the host. And it was so, when Gideon heard the telling of the dream, and the interpretation thereof, that he worshipped" (verses 13-15).

Gideon not only worshipped God for Himself and for the deliverance He was about to accomplish on behalf of His people; he worshipped Him for the method by which He was going to achieve His purpose. It is the means it pleased God to use in the overthrow of the Midianites that is so arresting here. In this situation it is the amazing way God worked to reach His end that draws us out in worship. Praise God, when we have no way out it is always an easy matter for Him to open a way; and though it seemed absurd to expect 300 men to overthrow the vast Midianite host, yet that was the way God chose to work deliverance for His people and to get glory for Himself. Please remember that God craves worship from His children for that is the thing that supremely glorifies Him.

WORSHIPPING GOD FOR THE GIFT OF A CHILD

In I Samuel chapter 1 we truly meet the spirit of

worship. You recall the story. Peninnah had children, but Hannah was barren, "and her rival provoked her sore, for to make her fret." Hannah in her distress besought the Lord for a son, and her request was granted. As soon as the child was weaned she brought him to the temple in Shiloh and presented him there with these words: "For this child I prayed; and the Lord hath given me my petition which I asked of Him: therefore I also have granted him to the Lord; as long as he liveth he is granted to the Lord." Did you note two phrases here? To me they are exceedingly precious. Read them together. "The Lord hath given me . . . I also have granted . . . to the Lord. The Lord gave the child to her, and she gave the child back to Him. What answer to prayer surpasses this one? The sum total of her request was for this child, and when she had received all she craved she gave all back to the Giver.

Brothers and Sisters, of a person such as this it can be truly written that she "worshipped the Lord." It is not the person who wants God's grace, but the person who wants God Himself, who can worship Him worthily. Hannah shows us what was supremely precious to her — not the answer to prayer, not the grace given, but God's way with her in the giving of His gift. God gave Samuel to her, and she gave Samuel to God; and as Samuel passed out of her hands into God's hands, worship issued from her heart to God's heart. And not until our Samuel has passed out of our hands into the hands of God shall we begin to know the meaning of worship.

I can never forget Abraham. We have referred to him frequently of late, but I cannot refrain from mentioning him again. I never cease to be impressed by the preciousness of his remark to his servants when he was on his way to offer up Isaac. "I and the lad will go yonder; and we will worship." To Abraham the offering up of his son was not a matter of sacrifice, it was a matter of worship. For him to worship God was to give his son to God. Abraham recognised this as God's Way of receiving worship, so he offered worship in the way that God desired.

Brothers and Sisters, I do not believe that anyone who has not consecrated his all on God's altar can really worship Him. We may try to do so, but we cannot do so in truth. But when the day comes for me, as it came for Hannah, that my Samuel, in whom all my hopes are centred, passes out of my hands into God's hands, then worship will flow out to God with the out-going of my son. True worship is found in one place only — at the altar. When our hands are emptied of all we hold dear, the focus shifts from self to God, and that is worship. Worship always follows in the wake of the Cross, for there God is All and in all. It is necessary therefore that Samuel pass out of our hands.

WORSHIPPING GOD FOR HIS VINDICATION
OF HIMSELF

God's ways do not always involve His answer to prayers. The reverse often holds good. God's ways do not always mean our prosperity; not infrequently they bring adversity. What should be our attitude then?

In II Samuel chapter 12 we have the record of David's sin in connection with Bathsheba. God sent the prophet Nathan to him with the message that the child would surely die. David had sinned, but he loved his son though the child was the fruit of his sin. He had a father's heart, and he pled with God for his life. But God had said, "Because by this deed thou hast given great occasion to the enemies of the Lord to blaspheme, the child also that is born unto thee shall surely die." Nevertheless, when the child sickened David sought the Lord in prayer. And he knew how to pray; we see that in the Psalms. David not only prayed, he fasted, and all night long he lay prostrate on the ground before God. But the child died! Anyone who was not truly in subjection to God, after seeking Him with such intensity, would have charged Him with harshness when his request was not granted. Many Christians have a controversy with God when His ways conflict with their ways. Not so David. Others might rebel; not he. Others might lose heart; not he. When the child died his servants feared to break the news to him. They reasoned among themselves that if David was almost overwhelmed with anxiety when the child fell sick, his grief would be insupportable when he learned of the child's death. What actually happened? "Then David arose from the earth, and washed, and anointed himself, and changed his apparel; and he came into the house of the Lord, and worshipped: then he came to his own house; and when he required they set bread before him, and he did eat."

What is worship? It is bowing to the ways of God. It is not a dull kind of submission. It is not lapsing into hopelessness or passivity. It is a positive recognition of the rightness of God's ways.

It is often necessary for God to vindicate Himself in relation to us. Do you understand what that means? When we sin He has to justify Himself by making it clear to the angels, to the devil, to the world and to all his children that He has no part in our sin. He has to make it plain to principalities and powers, to the world and to the Church that He cannot be involved in our iniquity. When we are found guilty before Him He does not let us off. His governmental hand comes upon us and we are tried in the fires of affliction. How do we react at such a time? Those who know and love God say to Him then: "If my affliction can vindicate Thy holiness, then I say, Amen. If Thou canst make known Thy righteousness by my suffering, then I acknowledge that Thou doest all things well. If in this way Thy nature can be vindicated, I gladly accept Thy dealings with me."

Please note that David was a normal human being. God's Word constantly depicts people's inner feelings, and it shows us how human David was. He was not devoid of natural affection. He loved his child and he prayed for his child. Some people are such very special beings; they are super-spiritual and do not seem to live on this earthly plane. David was a normal person and he felt the death of his child keenly; but when he saw the hand of God in this, he bowed before Him in worship.

May God deliver us from our controversies with Him! When we meet with disappointment and frustration we shall worship Him if we see His ways. O Brothers and Sisters, let me say yet again that not a soul can truly worship God who does not bow to His ways. If we are to worship Him, revelation is a basic condition: if we are to worship His ways, subjection is a basic condition. Apart from revelation we cannot worship God Himself: apart from subjection we cannot worship His ways. We need to be brought to the point where we say to Him: "Lord, I am willing to submit to Thee even if that which I hold dearest is taken away. Such submission is worship.

I count it the greatest blessing of my life to have known Miss Barber. Scores of times, perhaps even hundreds of times, I have heard her say: "Lord, I praise Thee for Thy ways." Hers were no superficial prayers.

They came from the depths of her being and were often uttered when she was suffering intensely. God's ways do not always mean a prospering of our ways, nor do they always bring answers to our agonised pleading, not even when we plead with fasting. But if the child we love is taken from us, let us still adore His ways.

WORSHIPPING GOD WHEN DEPRIVED OF EVERYTHING

Finally let us look at another illustration of the ways of God, not, as in the case of David, when God's holiness demanded His vindication because of sin that had not been dealt with; but in the case of Job, whom God in the mystery of His ways permitted to be deprived of everything he possessed, though He Himself had just borne witness of him that there was "none like him in the earth, a perfect and an upright man" (Job 1.8).

Job was a wealthy man. He was rich in sheep, and camels and cattle. And Job had many children. One day a messenger suddenly appeared on the scene with the news that all his cattle had been carried off by the Sabeans. Before he had finished speaking a second person brought the report that the fire of God had fallen from heaven and devoured all his sheep. And while the second messenger was still telling his tale of woe, a third arrived to intimate a further calamity. The Chaldeans, he said, had carried off all Job's camels.

Before the third messenger had ended his tale a fourth brought the tragic news that every one of his children had perished. A gale from the desert had caused the house to collapse while they were feasting together, and they were all buried under the wreckage. These four different messengers, arriving almost simultaneously, brought home to Job the grim fact that by disaster upon disaster, within the scope of one short day, he had been stripped bare of everything he possessed. How did he react? "Then Job arose, and rent his mantle, and shaved his head, and fell down upon the ground, and worshipped; and he said, Naked came I out of my mother's womb, and naked shall I return thither: the Lord gave, and the Lord hath taken away; blessed be the name of the Lord" (verses 20-21).

Job's first act was to worship God. And do be clear on this point, that in Job's case there was no question of God having to vindicate Himself because of sin in the life. It was purely a question of God acting as He deemed well. Though Job, in a matter of hours, had been bereft of his all, he could instantly fall down and worship God. Here was a man so utterly subject to God, that he could unhesitatingly bow to all God's ways.

Brothers and Sisters, God has been working in many of your lives, stripping you through adversity of much that you have cherished. What is your reaction to His dealings? Do you keep comparing your lot with the lot of others, wondering why they are prospered while your experience is one of trial upon trial? Oh, that you might cease from all your reasonings and submit to the Lord! Oh, that you might yield under the pressure of His hand! Then you would begin to discover him in your business, in all your associations in all your circumstances, in all your prosperity and in all your adversity. When you bow to His ways you will know what it means to worship Him.

Where there is true worship there are no complaints. In the first chapter of Job we see worship in deed and in truth. Whatever God's dealings with you may be, whether they seem reasonable or unreasonable, they are invariably good. In David's case they were reasonable, for he had sinned. But at times, as in the case of Job, they seem unreasonable. They cannot be accounted for by sin in the life, nor by lack of spirituality. But when His dealings with us are inexplicable, let us fall before Him and acknowledge that He does all things well; even His very best He is not withholding from us. May He grant us grace from this day forth to offer Him not only the worship that is begotten of revelation, but the worship that expresses itself in an unreserved acceptance of His ways. May we learn these two aspects of worship and be those who worship Him for what He has by revelation made known of Himself, and worship Him also by our glad submission to His ways with us. May He find us those who, no matter how He may choose to deal with us, always look up to Him and say: "Thy

ways with me are right ways, eternally right. Not a
thing that has befallen me has been to my hurt. I
thank Thee for the frustration of my ways that I might
know Thy ways." Let us cease questioning God's
dealings with us and with our brothers and sisters. And
let us cease asking for any explanation of His dealings,
however baffling they may be. Let us in simplicity of
heart accept it as a settled fact that all His ways are
higher than our ways, and all His ways are perfect.

May we one and all be saved from our controversies
and questionings and be brought to a place of such
submission that we become His footstool. "Lord, grant
it for Thine own Name's sake! Amen!"

CHAPTER NINE

THE KEY TO PRAYER

"He that seeketh findeth." (Matt.7.8) "I have set watchmen upon thy walls, O Jerusalem; they shall never hold their peace day nor night: ye that are the Lord's remembrancers, take ye no rest, and give him no rest, till he establish, and till he make Jerusalem a praise in the earth." (Isaiah.62.6, 7)

In the spiritual life of a Christian prayer is a matter of great importance. Every true Christian realises this and gives himself to prayer. And yet, though some of the Lord's children spend time praying over many matters, they do not seem to get through in prayer. The reason is that they have not discovered the key.

No matter what we take in hand to do, we need to know how to do it. It is this know-how that is so important. If we want to enter a room and the door is locked, we can find no way in unless we possess the key. Or if we want to carry a table through a door, provided we know how to go about it, we shall carry it in without a hitch; but if we do not know how to handle things, we shall carry it awkwardly, bumping and banging in a vain effort to get it through the door. The trouble is not the

weight of the table, nor is it the width of the door; it is
the lack of this know-how on the part of those who are
doing the job. People who have learned the art of doing
things do things well: people who have not learned the
art labour in vain.

So it is with prayer. Matt. 7 speaks of principles
relating to prayer, one of which is "He that seeketh
findeth." Seeking requires time. Anyone who looks for
a thing in a half-hearted, easy-going manner is not likely
to find it. Seeking involves patience and perseverance,
and unless we are thorough-going we shall not find what
we seek. If God does not answer our prayers, we must
exercise patience and diligently seek the key to prayer.

The reason why God answered the prayers of many
of the saints in past days is that they had the key to prayer.
If you read the biography of George Muller you will see
that throughout his entire life he was always receiving
answers to prayer. George Muller had discovered the key.
Many earnest Christians pray at great length; they pray
wordy prayers, but they do not receive answers from God.
In prayer words are essential, but we must not be wordy.
Our words must be to the point; they should be words
that touch the heart of God and so move Him that they
leave Him no alternative but to grant our requests.
Words that are to the point are the key to prayer. Such
words are in perfect keeping with God's will, therefore
He cannot but respond to them. Let us look at a few
scriptural illustrations that we may learn the art of prayer.

ABRAHAM'S PRAYER

(Gen. 18.16-33)

When God had made it known to Abraham that He was about to execute judgment on Sodom and Gomorrah because of their wickedness, Abraham still waited before God. Then he began to pray for Sodom. He did not just open his mouth and say: "O God, have mercy on Sodom!" He did not with great intensity beseech God saying: "Oh, forbid that Sodom should be destroyed!" Abraham laid hold on the fact that God is a righteous God; and that was the key to prayer concerning Sodom. In deep humility and with great earnestness he proceeded to ask God one question after another. His questions were his requests. And as he proceeded in prayer he stood steadfastly on the ground of God's righteousness. At length he said: "Oh let not the Lord be angry, and I will speak yet but this once: peradventure ten shall be found there." That was Abraham's final request. After God answered it we are told that "the Lord went his way." Abraham did not try to hold on to God; he did not try to go on praying. We read, "Abraham returned unto his place." Some people say he should have continued beseeching God, but the Scriptures show that Abraham knew God, and he knew the art of prayer. He had heard the Lord say: "The cry of Sodom and Gomorrah is great and ... their sin is very grievous ... the cry of it is come unto me."

If there are not so many as ten righteous persons in a city, what kind of a city is it! Heb.1.9 tells us that the Lord loves righteousness and hates iniquity. He cannot cover sin and refrain from judgment. The destruction of Sodom and Gomorrah was the awful consequence of their sin, and it was the manifestation of God's righteousness. When He overthrew those cities He did no injustice to a single righteous person; He "delivered righteous Lot, sore distressed by the lascivious life of the wicked." (II Pet. 2.7) Abraham's prayer which was to the point was answered. There was no unrighteousness with God. He did not "consume the righteous with the wicked." We worship and we praise Him.

JOSHUA'S PRAYER ABOUT AI
(Josh.7)

When the children of Israel attacked the city of Ai "they fled before the men of Ai. And the men of Ai smote of them about thirty and six men: and they chased them from before the gate even unto Shebarim, and smote them at the going down: and the hearts of the people melted and became as water." How had it come about that after so mighty a triumph at Jericho the children of Israel suffered dire defeat at Ai? There was only one thing Joshua could do. Prostrating himself before the Lord, he enquired into the cause of this defeat. Naturally Joshua was grieved on account of the danger into which Israel had fallen; but what grieved him more was the dishonour that had been brought to the name of the Lord, therefore he enquired: "What wilt thou do for thy great name?" This was the key to his prayer. He honoured the name of God. His concern was what God would do for the sake of His own name. And God answered Joshua's enquiry. He said: "Israel hath sinned ... therefore the children of Israel cannot stand before their enemies ... I will not be with you any more except ye destroy the devoted thing from among you." God was concerned for His own name and could not therefore tolerate sin among His people. He heard Joshua's prayer and instructed him to discover and do away with the sin that had caused the trouble. When Joshua was clear about the reason for Israel's defeat, he rose up early in the morning to deal with the matter and discovered that the trouble was Achan's sin of covetousness. When all Israel had dealt with this sin their defeat was turned into victory. To tolerate sin is to cause God's name to be blasphemed and to give Satan occasion to attack God's people. When Joshua prayed about the defeat at Ai he did not just open his mouth in undiscerning zeal and plead with God to save His people and make them victorious. It was the dishonour brought upon God's name that grieved him, and his plea was that God would take up the case for His own name's sake. His prayer touched the crux of the matter and consequently brought an answer from

going." If our Lord as Man on the earth, possessing the key to prayer, had in this deliberate way to set aside His own will and seek the will of God, how dare we at random utter a few words in prayer and conclude we have discerned God's will?

THE PRAYER OF A CANAANITE
(Matt. 15.22-28; Mk.7.24-30)

This Canaanitish woman was in distress, and she cried out in her need: "Have mercy on me, O Lord, thou son of David." Was she not earnest in prayer? Truly she was. But the amazing thing is that the Lord "answered her not a word." And the disciples seemed to be in sympathy with the Lord, for they said to Him, "Send her away, for she crieth after us." But how did our Lord reply to them? He said, "I was not sent but unto the lost sheep of the house of Israel." That reply of the Lord's enabled the woman to discover the right approach to Him. She saw that the son of David was only related to the house of Israel, not to the nations. So she came and worshipped Him saying, "Lord, help me!" She now called Him "Lord", not "Son of David". She realised that only the house of Israel had a right to use that title, so she forsook the wrong ground on which she had been standing and addressed her prayer to Him as Lord. This prayer brought His answer — "It is not meet to take the children's bread and cast it to the dogs." The answer seemed so cold, it sounded as though the Lord was rejecting the woman. Actually He was seeking to show her where she stood so that she might know the meaning of grace. The woman saw her own place and saw also the grace of the Lord, and having now the key to prayer, she said: "Yea, Lord: for even the dogs eat of the crumbs which fall from their master's table." This called forth the Lord's commendation and He said to her, "O woman, great is thy faith!" It was because she had found the key that she quite naturally exercised faith. In Mk.7 we read that the Lord said, "For this saying go thy way; the devil is gone out of thy daughter." Her brief prayer was answered because she possessed the key and prayed to the point. This is what we need to learn. Often we put forth tremendous effort in prayer without getting any answer from God, yet we do not seek to discover why. Brothers and Sisters, how can we expect God to answer prayers that are wide of the mark? In all our praying we must first find the key, for only as we do so can we expect to have constant answers from God.

Having looked at these illustrations relating to prayer, let us bear in mind that we should heed the inner voice and not be governed by our circumstances, or thoughts, or affections. When that still small voice within tells us to pray, when in the deeps of our being we have a sense that we should pray, then let us respond at once. Circumstances should only be a means of driving

CHAPTER TEN

BURDEN AND PRAYER

"Thus saith the Lord that doeth it, the Lord that formeth it to establish it; the Lord is his name: Call unto me, and I will answer thee, and will shew thee great things and difficult, which thou knowest not." (Jer. 33. 2,3.) "Quench not the Spirit." (I Thess. 5.19)

I

Every child of God ought to have some God-given burden. But burdens can only be received from God as our spirits are open to Him. Openness of spirit to God is the condition of receiving burdens from God. And having received such burdens, we must learn to discharge them faithfully through prayer. When we have discharged the first burden we shall receive a second, and when the second is discharged we shall receive a third.

The matter of primary importance here is to open our spirits to God. Because of unfaithfulness we can easily reach a state where we receive no burdens at all, so if we wish to be those who bear God's burdens, we must be very sensitive and not reject any impression that comes from Him. At the outset such impressions may be faint, but they will gain in strength as we go on. If we quench the Spirit and lose our burden, the only way of recovery 'is to confess our sin and thereafter to respond faithfully to every God-given impression. As soon as you are moved to pray, pray. The sole reason for not receiving further burdens is that you have not released the burden you already have. Unload that, and burden after burden will follow as you unload. Be faithful. As you faithfully discharge the burden you have God will continuously given you further burdens to bear. Oh, Brothers and Sisters, if you hope to be of any use to God you must recover your lost burden.

Burdens are specially related to the work of God. Therefore, if we are seeking to do His will we must wait on Him till He communicates His burden to us, for His burden is the indication of His will. It is through the burdens He puts upon us that we discern His will for us and the way in which His will can be wrought out through our lives.

For instance, if God gives you a burden to preach the gospel, the more you preach the gospel the more you will come into release, whereas if you fail to discharge your burden it will weigh you down more and more till you are crushed beneath it. Then a barrier will arise between you and God and you will find it difficult to get in touch with Him.

Burdens of this nature are connected with all spiritual work. Try to work without a burden and your

every God-given burden, lest by violating the registrations He gives we lose our communion with Him and are crushed by the very burdens which, had we released them in prayer, would have brought our own release.

III

While it is true that the burdens we receive as we wait on God express His will for us, it is also true that in the main it is our knowledge which governs our burdens initially. There are exceptions. For instance, in the middle of the night God may call you to get up and pray for a brother in a remote place whose circumstances at that particular time are unknown to you, and not till later do you learn of the specific need he was in just then. But more often our burdens arise in connection with matters about which we have some information. God first brings a certain matter to our knowledge, and then on the basis of that knowledge a burden lodges.

IV

In connection with this ministry of prayer, which is of such importance to the Christian, a question arises: Does the exercise of our ministry call for utterance, or can we just bear our burdens silently before God?

We believe that if God gives a prayer burden then He wants it to be uttered. He wants audible expression given to it, however few and however disjointed the words may be. No burden can be discharged without expression. Brothers and Sisters, in the spiritual realm there is an amazing principle connected with this matter of utterance. God not only takes account of what we believe, He takes account of what we say. Mk. 6.29 records that our Lord said to the Syrophoenician woman: "For this saying go thy way; the devil is gone out of thy daughter." The woman spoke only a sentence, but the few words she uttered caused the Lord to work. We may make a request in our hearts, but there is more effect in an uttered request. God seems to require that we speak out what is in the heart. When our Lord was in the garden of Gethsemane, He was so heavily burdened that He "offered up prayers and supplications with strong crying" (Heb. 5.7). We are not insisting on loud prayers, but there should be a correspondence between the inner burden and the outward expression. If we cannot pray aloud in our homes, let us try and find a place of prayer elsewhere as the Lord did. He resorted to the desert (Mk. 1.3) and to the mountain (Lk. 6.12). At all events, let us pray audibly, even if we have to pray in a low voice. The burden God has given us has to be uttered in order to be released.

But our difficulty very often is that even when we are conscious of bearing a burden, and actually kneel down to pray, we are still unable to give expression to it. We know that something weighs on our spirits, but what that thing is we do not know. We need to realise that our burden is a matter of the spirit, whereas

needs the co-operation of His church on the earth, and it is through prayer that we co-operate with Him. May we provide Him a way for the outworking of His will!

CHAPTER ELEVEN

THE LIFE OF THE ALTAR AND THE TENT

Scripture Reading: Genesis 12.4, 8; 13.3, 4, 18.

The life of a Christian is the life of the altar and the tent. God requires of His children that in His presence they have an altar and that on the earth they have a tent. An altar calls for a tent, and a tent in turn demands an altar. It is impossible to have an altar without a tent, and likewise impossible to have a tent without a return to the altar. The altar and the tent are interrelated; the two cannot be divorced.

THE LIFE OF THE ALTAR

Gen. 12.7 reads: "The Lord appeared unto Abram and said, Unto thy seed will I give this land: and there builded he an altar unto the Lord who appeared unto him." Here we see that the altar is based on divine revelation. Where there is no revelation there is no altar. Unless God has appeared to a man that man cannot offer his all to God. It requires revelation to produce consecration. No man on his own initative can present himself to God. Man cannot come over to God's side.

But the day a man is met by God, that day consecration takes place in his life. If you get a sight of God you are no longer your own.

We need to realise that the power to offer oneself to God comes through revelation. Not all who preach consecration are consecrated people. Not all who understand the doctrine of consecration know the reality of consecration. Only those who have seen God are consecrated persons. God appeared to Abraham, and the immediate issue was that Abraham built an altar to God. The Lord Jesus appeared to Paul on the road to Damascus and Paul immediately asked: "Lord, what wilt Thou have me to do?" (Acts 22.10) A turning point in our spiritual history does not come through our decision to do something for God; it comes when we see Him. When we meet God a radical change takes place in the life. We can no longer do what we did in the past. When I meet Him Himself, then I have the power to deny myself. The matter of denying self ceases to be optional when we have met God. "No man can see God and live." If God appears to any man, the whole course of his life is altered. Oh! it is not my decision to serve the Lord that enables me to serve Him. It is not my will to build an altar that produces an altar. It is when God comes out to a man that an altar is built.

When God appeared to Abraham He said to him: "Unto thy seed will I give this land." Divine revelation brings us into a new inheritance. It brings the realisation that the Holy Spirit has been given to us now as an earnest of the inheritance which later on we shall possess in fulness.

God appeared to Abraham, and Abraham built an altar. This altar was not for sin offering, but for burnt offering. It was not a matter of settling the sin question, but of offering the life to God. It was the kind of altar spoken of in Rom. 12.1: "I beseech you therefore, brethren, by the mercies of God, to present your bodies a living sacrifice, holy, acceptable to God, which is your reasonable service." It was the mercy of God that caused the Lord Jesus to die for us: it was the mercy of God that provided the Cross on which we died with Him and on which the devil was dealt with: it is by the mercy of God that we have His life within: and it is the mercy of God that will bring us through to glory. It is on the ground of His mercies that God beseeches us to offer ourselves a living sacrifice to Him.

Note in connection with the burnt offering that while a person of ample resource might offer a bullock, one with less resource might offer a sheep, and one whose means was still more limited might offer a dove. (Lev.1.3,10,14) But whatever the offering, the offerer had to offer up the whole. God cannot accept less than an utter consecration.

And for what purpose is the burnt offering placed on the altar? To be wholly burnt. Many of us think we offer ourselves to God to do this or that for Him, whereas what He is wanting of us is not our work, but ourselves. What the altar signifies is not doing for God, but being for God. Unlike the sacrifice of the Old Testament, which in one act was finally burnt, the sacrifice of the New Testatment is "a living sacrifice." The meaning of the altar is the offering up of the life to God to be ever consumed, yet ever living: to be ever living, yet ever consumed. God wants these lives of ours consecrated to Him that throughout their entire course they may be ceaselessly being consumed for Him.

God appeared to Abraham, and Abraham offered himself to God. Abraham had not heard a lot of doctrine about consecration, nor had he been urged by others to consecrate himself; but Abraham had seen God, and when that happened he immediately built an altar to God. Oh, Brothers and Sisters, consecration is a spontaneous thing! Anyone to whom God has manifested Himself cannot do other than live for Him. So it was with Abraham, and so it has been with everyone who has met God throughout the two thousand years of church history.

THE LIFE OF THE TENT

The altar has its issue in the tent. Gen.12.8 says: "And he removed from thence unto the mountain on the east of Bethel, and pitched his tent." From now on Abraham lives in a tent. Actually he lived in a tent before, but not until he had built the altar does the Word of God bring the tent into view.

What is a tent? A tent is not a settled abode, it is moveable. Through the altar God deals with ourselves; through the tent God deals with our possessions. At the altar Abraham had offered up his all to God. Was he thereafter stripped of everything? No! Abraham still possessed cattle and sheep and many other things; but he had become a tent-dweller. In other words, what was not consumed on the altar became attached to the tent. When we place our all on the altar, God claims many of our possessions, but what He leaves for our use belongs to the tent.

Abraham's life was a life of the altar. A day came when even his only begotten son was offered upon it. But what did God do with Isaac? He restored him to Abraham. What you place on the altar God accepts. He cannot allow you to live for your own pleasure. The altar claims your all, and while God restores certain things from the altar, they can no longer be regarded as your own; they are related to the tent.

Some people ask: If I give my all to God, do I not have to sell all my possessions and dispose of all my money? If I consecrate myself to God, how much furniture may I have in my home and how many garments in my wardrobe? Some people are truly perplexed over such questions. But we need to remember that we have

a life to live before God, and we have also a life to live
in the world. In our life before God all must truly be
on the altar, but for our life in the world we still have
need of many material things. We need clothing, and
food and a dwelling-place. We ought to consecrate our
all to God and live for Him alone; but if He says I may
retain a certain thing, then I retain it. Nevertheless,
we must apply the principle of the tent to such things
as He permits us to retain, for they are given back to
us to meet our need in the world. We may use them,
but we must not be governed by them. We can have
them, or we can let them go; they can be given, and they
can be taken away. This is the principle of tent-life.
Let us learn this lesson, that we dare not use anything
that has not been placed on the altar, neither may we
take anything back from the altar, and what God gives
back must be held on the principle of the tent.

THE SECOND ALTAR

Gen. 12,8 says: "And he removed from thence unto
the mountain on the east of Bethel, and pitched his tent,
having Bethel on the west and Ai on the east: and there
he builded an altar unto the Lord." This is Abraham's
second altar. The altar had led to the tent, and now
the tent leads again to the altar. If our possessions
are not held loosely on the principle of the tent, they
will cause us to take root, and there will never be a

second altar. When we have consecrated our all to God, He lets us use certain things in the tent; but we have no choice as to what we take there. Everything must pass the altar that goes into the tent, and what has been placed in the tent may have to go to the alter again. At any time God may say: "I want this thing." If we cling to it and say: "This is mine," then in heart we have forsaken the altar and cannot say to God that our life is being lived for Him. We may have built our first altar, but in process of time we may have accumulated many things that cause us to depart from the life of the tent. If so, there can be no further altar. But how precious it is if we can always be tent-dwellers and can build a second altar.

THE RECOVERY OF THE ALTAR
AND THE TENT

Abraham had his failures. In his history there was a forsaking of the altar and the tent. But there was recovery. How did that recovery come about? Gen. 13.3-4 tells us: "He went on his journeys from the South even to Bethel, unto the place where his tent had been at the beginning, between Bethel and Ai; unto the place of the altar which he had made there at the first: and there Abram called on the name of the Lord." Recovery is a matter of returning to the altar and the tent.

Have any of you failed? Have any of you gone

down into Egypt, so that now you have your own interests and your own aspirations? If you are seeking the way of recovery, you will find it at the altar and in the tent. Abraham's recovery involved his return "unto the place where his tent had been ... unto the place of the alta: which he had made." But what happened to Abraham after his recovery? Gen.8.18 records: "Abram moved his tent, and came and dwelt by the oaks of Mamre which are in Hebron, and built there an altar unto the Lord." Hebron means "fellowship." After his recovery Abraham entered into the place of continuous fellowship with God. And Abraham built another altar. If we are in fellowship with God we will never forsake the altar. May He be gracious to us and cause us to see the importance of consecration so that we may live a life of the altar and the tent!

CHAPTER TWELVE

DEEP CALLETH UNTO DEEP

Scripture Reading: Ps. 42.7; Mk. 4.5, 6; Matt. 5.14-16;
6.1-6; Isa. 39.1-6; 2 Cor. 12.1-4;
Acts 5.1-5.

Ps. 42.7 reads: "Deep calleth unto deep." Only a call from the depths can provoke a response from the depths: only that which springs from the deeps of your own being will have a deep effect on the lives of others. You yourself derive little help from shallow preaching, and you in turn can offer little real help to others unless your own life has been deeply affected. What is superficial will never produce anything other than superficial results. Yes, you may be able to stir the emotions of others by your tears or smiles: you may even stimulate enthusiasm and produce temporary results: but if you lack depth you will never be able to touch the deeps in other souls.

DEEP ROOTS

In the parable of the sower the Lord Jesus speaks of some seed which fell on "rocky ground where it had not much earth; and straightway it sprang up because it had no deepness of earth: and when the sun was risen, it was scorched; and because it had no root, it withered away (Mk. 4.5, 6).

What is root? It is growth beneath the soil. What are leaves? Growth above the soil. Root is hidden life: leaves are manifest life. The trouble with many Christians is that, while there is much apparent life, there is very little secret life.

You have been a Christian for a number of years, have you not? Then let me ask: How much of your life is hidden from view? How much is unknown to others? You stress outward works. Yes, good works are important; but apart from that manifest expression of your life, how much of your life remains hidden? If all your spiritual life is exposed, then all your growth is upward, and because there is no downward growth you lack root.

In our Christian life it is necessary that we learn the meaning of the Body of Christ; we must learn to live corporately. On the other hand, we must learn that the life given to each member of His Body by the Lord is distinctly individual; and that measure given to you personally by Him needs to be guarded, otherwise it will lose its specific character and will be of no particular use to Him. If that which has been specially committed to you is exposed it will wither.

The discourse of the Lord Jesus on the Mount was most remarkable. On the one hand He said: "Ye are the light of the world. A city set on a hill can not be hid ... Let your light shine before men, that they may see your good works and glorify your Father which is in heaven" (Matt. 5.14-16). On the other hand He said: "Take heed that ye do not your righteousness before men, to be seen of them ... But when thou doest alms, let not thy left hand know what thy right hand doeth: that thine alms may be in secret ... When thou prayest, enter into thine inner chamber, and having shut thy door, pray to thy Father which is in secret" (Matt. 6. 1-6).

On the one hand, if you are a Christian you must come right out into the open and make a public profession: on the other hand, there are Christian virtues which you should preserve from the public gaze. The Christian who parades all his virtues has no depth, and because he lacks root he will not be able to stand in the day of trial and temptation. Let us who have been the Lord's children these many years ask Him to show us to what extent our experiences have become exposed to view, and let us ask Him also to work a work in these lives of ours that will ensure our becoming deeply rooted in Him.

DEEP EXPERIENCES

Writing to the Corinthians, Paul said: "I must needs glory, though it is not expedient" (2 Cor. 12.1). He admitted that for himself it was "unprofitable"

(Gk.) to glory in his experiences; but for the sake of
others he was obliged to speak of "visions and revelations of the Lord." Alas! many of us cannot stand the
test of visions and revelations: as soon as we have a little
experience everyone knows about it.

It was necessary for Paul to mention his experiences,
but when he referred to them, did he disclose everything?
Far from it. This is how he wrote — "I know a man
in Christ, fourteen years ago (whether in the body, I
know not; or whether out of the body, I know not;
God knoweth), such a one caught up even to the third
heaven." The man to whom Paul referred was himself,
and this experience of being raptured to the third
heaven had taken place fourteen years previously. What
depth there was in Paul! For fourteen years he had
never divulged his experience: for fourteen years God's
Church knew nothing of it: for fourteen years not one
of the Apostles had heard of it. Paul's roots had struck
deep beneath the soil.

Some people would be inclined to say: "Paul, you
let us hear all about that experience of yours fourteen
years ago: it would be most helpful for us to know the
whole story." But note how indefinitely Paul speaks of
himself and his experience — "I know such a man
(whether in the body, or apart from the body, I know
not; God knoweth), how that he was caught up into
Paradise, and heard unspeakable words which it is not
lawful for a man to utter." Right up to the present day

that experience of Paul's has not been uprooted.

Brothers and Sisters, this matter of root is a matter of extreme importance. If you want to have Paul's ministry, then you need to have Paul's "root": if you want to have Paul's outward conduct, then you need to have Paul's inner life: if you want to have Paul's manifest power, then you need to have Paul's secret experience. The trouble with Christians today is that they cannot keep any spiritual experience undisclosed. As soon as they have a little bit of experience they have to tell it abroad: they have to live their lives in the limelight; they have to uproot everything. May God lead us to strike our roots more deeply!

SUPERFICIAL LIVING

In Isaiah chapter 39 we are told that when the news of Hezekiah's sickness and recovery reached the Babylonian court, messengers were dispatched with letters and a present for Hezekiah. Hezekiah had been a recipient of the grace of God, but he was unable to stand the test of grace. God's Word says: "And Hezekiah was glad of them, and showed them the house of his precious things, the silver, and the gold, and the spices, and the precious oil, and all the house of his armour, and all that was found in his treasures." Hezekiah could not overcome the temptation to display everything. He had just been wonderfully healed of his sickness, and no doubt felt self-important and thought there were few people in the world who had had such a remarkable experience as he. To how many had God given so marvellous a sign at their healing as to him when the shadow on the dial of Ahaz went back ten degrees? In his elation Hezekiah displayed all his treasures to the men from Babylon, so that everything he possessed was known to them. Because of this exposure Isaiah said to him: "Hear the word of the Lord of hosts. Behold, the days come, that all that is in thine house, and that which thy fathers have laid up in store until this day, shall be carried to Babylon: nothing shall be left, saith the Lord." The measure in which we display things to others will be the measure of our own loss. This is a solemn matter and it demands our attention.

Alas that so many people cannot forbear disclosing their experiences! A brother once said: "Lots of the brothers fall sick, and when they recover they give their testimonies. I wish I could develop some sickness — but not a fatal one — and that God would heal me; then I would have something to say at the next testimony meeting." What was this brother's motive? To be able to give a testimony. He sought an experience in order to have something to talk about. Oh! this superficial kind of living brings grave loss to God's children: it rules out the possibility of spiritual progress.

Then ought we not to bear testimony to God's grace? Yes, we ought. Paul did so; and multitudes of God's children from generation to generation have done so too. But to bear testimony is one thing: to delight in exposing one's experience is quite another thing. What is our object in testifying? Is it that others may be profited, or is it that we may have the pleasure of talking? 'The love of hearing one's own voice, and the desire to be helpful to others, are two totally different things. We need not refrain from testifying, but we must refrain from exposing everything.

The Lord Jesus sometimes gave His testimony, but He was never given to talking. In Mark's Gospel we are told on more than one occasion that He healed the sick and insisted that the story of the healing be kept secret. But in Mark 5.19 it is recorded that, after healing a demon-possessed man, He said to him: "Go to thy house unto thy friends, and tell them how great things the Lord has done for thee, and how he had mercy on thee." We may tell what great things the Lord has done for us, but we must not publish these things abroad as items of news; nor dare we disclose everything, for to do so is to lay bare our roots. It is essential that some of our experiences remain covered: to uncover all is to lose all.

And let us remember that if we display all our treasure, captivity cannot be averted. If we expose our roots, we shall find that we have exposed them to enemy attack, and God will not protect us. If He wants us to give a testimony, we have no alternative but to disclose that particular experience of His grace that He asks for, but our many other experiences must remain hidden.

The same applies to our work. By His grace God has accomplished something through us, but do remember that what He has accomplished is not matter for advertisement or propaganda. If we expose the work of God we shall find that the touch of death will come upon it immediately; and the loss will correspond to the extent to which we uncover results. As soon as David numbered the children of Israel, death set in and many of the people perished (2 Sam. 24).

Our secret history with the Lord must be preserved, apart from that which He requires us to disclose. Only if He moves within us to reveal anything dare we reveal it. If He wants us to share some experience with a brother, we dare not withhold it, for that would be violating a law of the Body of Christ. Fellowship is a law of corporate life, so when the life rises within one member to flow out toward another, it must not be suppressed. We must be positive, not negative, and must always minister life to others. If we are engrossed the livelong day with our own experiences, and talk of them from morning to night, we expose ourselves to assault from the enemy. I trust we shall learn what the Body of Christ is, and what interflow of life among the members is; but I trust we shall also learn the need of safeguarding that which is specifically ours as members of the Body.

As your secret life deepens you will discover that "deep calleth unto deep." When you can bring forth values from the depths of your inner life, you will find that other lives will be deeply affected. Without any mighty outward movement — just a quiet response to the moving of life within — you will reach out to another life, and that other life will be helped, and into his life will come the awareness that in a depth deeper than consciousness he has met depth: deep has answered deep. If your life has no depth, your superficial work will only affect other lives superficially. We repeat yet again — only "deep calleth unto deep."

W. N. LITERATURE AVAILABLE

FROM

CHRISTIAN LITERATURE CRUSADE

⁂   ⁂   ⁂

Changed Into His Likeness

Love Not the World

Normal Christian Life

Normal Christian Worker

Selections from Normal Christian Life

Release of the Spirit

Sit, Walk, Stand

Song of Songs

Table in the Wilderness
     (Daily Devotional)

Twelve Baskets Full (Vol. 1)

Twelve Baskets Full (Vol. 2)

What Shall This Man Do?

Why This Waste?